Love in the Present Tense

"Any couple committed to learning and growing, individually as well as together, will find great tools in this book. Its message about the power of shared values is especially potent."

—Steve Gray, Managing Publisher,
The Christian Science Monitor

Bull Publishing Company
P.O. Box 1377
Boulder, CO 80304
800-676-2855
www.bullpub.com

ISBN 0-923521-81-X

Distributed to the trade by:
Publishers Group West
1700 Fourth Street
Berkeley, CA 94710

Library of Congress Cataloging-in-Publication Data

Shechtman, Morris R.
   Love in the present tense : how to have a high-intimacy, low-
maintenance marriage / by Morrie and Arleah Shechtman.
       p. cm.
Includes bibliographical references and index.
   ISBN 0-923521-81-X
   1. Marriage. 2. Man-woman relationships. I. Shechtman, Arleah. II.
Title.

   HQ734.S53 2003
   306.81—dc22
                                                    2003020369

How to Have a High-Intimacy,
Low-Maintenance Marriage

Love in the
Present Tense

Morrie and Arleah Shechtman

Bull Publishing Company
Boulder, Colorado

Contents

Introduction   *vi*

Chapter 1   *1*
Myth: Opposites attract—a couple, in their differences, complements each other.
Reality: Great relationships require identical core values.

Chapter 2   *23*
Myth: Love will carry you through the hard times in a relationship.
Reality: It is shared values that pull you through a crisis.

Chapter 3   *43*
Myth: You need to work on your marriage if you want it to be good.
Reality: Relationships don't have problems; people do.

Chapter 4   *67*
Myth: Selflessness and giving to others build the best relationships.
Reality: Clear limits and boundaries build mutual respect and lasting relationships.

Chapter 5   *95*
Myth: Unconditional acceptance of your partner is the foundation of a good marriage.
Reality: If you don't make demands on your partner, you don't really care.

Chapter 6   *115*
Myth: Frequent conflicts are a sign that a marriage is in trouble.
Reality: Your willingness to engage in conflict determines the depth and quality of your relationship.

Chapter 7   **145**
Myth: Spending lots of time together is very important.
Reality: The best relationships are low maintenance and
high intimacy.

Chapter 8   **163**
Myth: Trusting your partner is essential to a good
relationship.
Reality: It is trusting yourself that is essential.

Index   **181**

About the Authors   **187**

Acknowledgments   **188**

Introduction

You are not living in your parents' world. Yet many people are still trying to live (or live down) their parents' marriages. You might rush to deny this at first, pointing out that you're a two-career couple, that housework is shared (insofar as housework is actually getting done), that husband does not waltz in saying "Honey, I'm home" with any firm expectation of finding wife and meatloaf in the kitchen. Your outward arrangements are quite different, yet your sense of what marriage is supposed to be as an *inner* arrangement is deeply influenced by expectations you absorbed as a child. We carry into adulthood all sorts of unexamined assumptions about what marriage is supposed to feel like. Some of them may have been true for your ancestors but do not apply very well to the contemporary world. And some of them, quite frankly, were *never* true. Old wives have been dishing up baloney about love and marriage pretty much since time began.

Take, for example, the belief that if you want to be close to your partner, you need to spend lots of time together. If you're like most couples, you probably are not doing this. Instead, you are having fights about how you're not doing it. One of you is pressuring the other-or perhaps both of you are pressuring yourselves—to make more time. Most people imagine that this is a problem unique to contemporary American life with its high pressure jobs, long commuting distances, frequent business travel, and so forth. They imagine that prior to the invention of TVs, computers, cell phones, and two-career couples, married people used to spend vast tracks of time gazing into each other's eyes across candlelit tables. It isn't so. Never, in the entire history of the world has the average married couple had the leisure to spend hours hanging out alone together. To do so is unnecessary and, as we will go on to argue in Chapter 7, not even especially desirable.

Myths about marriage lead people to aim for unrealistic ideals and then to blame themselves and each other when they fall short. When mythical solutions fail to resolve mythical problems, when, despite your best efforts to apply the prescriptions of old wives and marriage counselors, you continue to experience pain in your marriage, you might be tempted to conclude that the marriage itself is hopeless. You might conclude that you've chosen the wrong partner or that you yourself are simply not cut out for marriage. This is rarely the case. In fact, most people choose exactly the right partner (albeit for all the wrong reasons). More often than not, it's your mythology and not your spouse that needs to be discarded.

We are not marriage counselors. Though we often work with married couples, we do not attempt to directly "fix" a marriage. Instead, we concentrate on the issues each spouse is grappling with as an individual. It is *people* not marriages that are happy or unhappy. What appears to be a marital problem is actually each person's individual unhappiness being aggravated by the other person's individual unhappiness. When the source of that personal unhappiness is addressed and healed, most couples are delighted to find that there is nothing seriously amiss with the marriage itself. They discover that they are quite capable of sorting out their everyday problems and conflicts without the assistance of a professional referee.

As psychotherapists, we are best known for our focus on personal growth in the workplace, and we do a lot of consulting for businesses. Our work with couples is more often than not the outgrowth of this consulting work. As executives open up about what is bothering them in their professional lives, they eventually come round to talking about their marriages as well and ask us to meet with their spouses.

Perhaps that strikes you as odd. A common misconception in our culture is that professional life and personal life can and should be kept in separate compartments. This notion bears little resemblance to how people actually live nowadays. Our work lives are no longer confined to the hours between 9 a.m. and 5 p.m., nor can the demands of our families always be postponed until after business hours. To believe you can make an *emotional* separation between the personal and the professional is just as unrealistic.

The marriages of our corporate clients are relevant to their professional lives because a happy marriage and a successful career require essentially the same inner resources. As we see it, companies and marriages founder for the same basic reason: the failure of the individuals within them to grow.

One reason people don't grow is that it has never occurred to them that they're supposed to. Until rather recently in human history, cultivating the inner life was a luxury most people neither wanted nor could afford. To survive in the past, all a person needed was a knack for something like hunting, gathering, farming, engineering, or accounting. Personal feelings were not especially relevant to any of these enterprises. A person was considered fully grown at the age of twenty-one. Whatever emotional maturity he'd attained by then was supposed to suffice for the rest of his adult life.

The basis of our economy has changed drastically over the past few decades and brought with it profound changes in lifestyle. To survive in this shifting economy, you've had to abandon assumptions about the world that seemed perfectly true and reliable when you were a child. Chances are that you are no longer using some of the skills that you expected to see you through a lifelong career. You have developed new skills only to find that these, too, rapidly became obsolete. By now you are realizing that skills alone are no guarantee of job security. What you need now is a knack for letting go of old knacks, a knack for recognizing and seizing new opportunities, and a knack for constantly reassessing what you have to offer and what you wish to receive. Your most essential skill is an ability to relate fully and accurately to what is going on *in the present.*

Your personal feelings are *highly* relevant to your ability to adapt in this way. To let go of the old and risk embracing the new is emotionally challenging. The less you can count on the external world remaining stable and consistent, the more you have to count on *yourself*. If you can't find your center and if you don't know and respect and trust yourself, then the ragged uncertainties of the new millennium will drive you batty.

Your partner, too, is living in this volatile world. She, too, must grow to survive in it. That means that neither you nor your partner are exactly the people you were when you got married—not if you're successful, at any rate. So your marriage itself requires constant adaptation. What works for you as a couple right now might not work for you a year from now. Personal growth alters your marriage, and changes in your marriage challenge you to further personal growth.

This book is about how to love in the perpetually shifting present. You may find it ironic, then, that so much of what we will say in it concerns the past. We will be encouraging you to explore your memories of childhood when you are having trouble in your marriage. That is because unexamined pain from the past amplifies and complicates pain in the present. It keeps us stuck in patterns of feeling and behaving that do not serve our adult relationships well.

The pop-psych version of this idea would have it that if you are unhappy as an adult, then your family of origin was dysfunctional and probably abusive. Bad feelings in the present can be traced to traumatic experiences in the past. The way to feel better is first to become enraged with your parents and then to forgive them completely and unconditionally.

That is not what we mean when we bring up your past. We believe that your feeling patterns as an adult were shaped by the way you felt on the *average* days of your childhood, days when nothing especially memorable or out of the ordinary occurred. The *familiar*—a mood or feeling that you never especially noticed because it was so habitual, so ordinary—shaped your expectations of what is ordinary to feel as an adult. In other words, you expect your life always to have the emotional texture you got used to when you were a child. When you feel like that now—even if it's not an especially good feeling—you feel safe.

Some of your familiars are positive. If your parents usually listened with interest when you had something to say, then you grew up taking it for granted that people would listen to you. To feel heard is what you consider normal. Maybe at some point you had a teacher who disparaged you for being outspoken. This event is memorable because it was so unusual and upsetting to you at the time. Nevertheless, it didn't lead you to become shy, precisely because it *was* unusual. The everyday experience of being heard is what shaped your expectations of the world.

If your parents offered you adequate protection, then you are used to a feeling of physical security. To feel safe is so normal for you that you probably don't even think about it. Perhaps there was one scary event from which you could not be shielded—a classmate was killed in an accident or a stranger exposed himself to you. This may be a vivid and upsetting memory, yet it probably didn't compromise your overall trust in the world because a feeling of safety was your *habitual* experience. To feel safe most of the time now that you are an adult is a gift that you got from your parents.

You also have negative familiars—feelings you might not even think of as especially negative because you're so used to them. If you got the impression that one or both of your parents disapproved of you when you expressed anger openly, then you probably learned to express it covertly, if at all. As an adult you can scarcely even conceive of raising your voice. Feeling ashamed of yourself the moment you are tempted to get angry is a familiar. You may have trouble even imagining that there might be other options.

Your most deeply rooted familiars can be traced to your relationships with your parents. Other childhood relationships may have been significant, memorable, and even formative, but relationships with parents are uniquely powerful in shaping our familiars. It is in relation to our parents that we get a sense of who we fundamentally are and what we can expect from others— a sense that develops long before we are able to think about it consciously. The familiar is based not so much on what our parents actually did but on the conclusions we drew about what they did.

A child's biggest fear is being abandoned. Children are keenly aware that they will not survive if their parents desert them. While few parents literally and permanently abandon their kids, many of us grew up *feeling* abandoned in some way. This is partly because the young are so helplessly dependent on their parents. Children feel abandoned anytime they don't get what they need from a parent because they have no other way of getting it. They may feel abandoned also because they have no perspective on time. An hour of being angry with a toddler may seem short to the mother, but to the toddler it is an eternity. A child that young doesn't yet have the experience to know that affection withdrawn for an hour has not been withdrawn forever.

All young children believe that they are the cause of what their parents are feeling and doing. When faced with what feels to them like abandonment, children blame themselves. They jump to strange conclusions about why they are to blame. If mother is prone to migraines and withdraws in pain when her child is playing noisily, then the child may infer that her own high spirits are the cause of her mother's headache. In the hope of preventing any more headaches, she learns to subdue her own glee and becomes perpetually sedate. As an adult, she is unable to get excited, and she has no idea why. She doesn't recall her childhood conclusion. Feeling subdued has become her familiar. She would say that it's just the way she is.

If you are a parent, the stories we will tell about our clients' familiars and how they arose may worry you. You will read of one person who suffers as an adult from having received too much parental feedback and another who suffers from having received too little. One was wounded by a dictatorial father, another by a father who wouldn't set limits at all. You may begin to get the impression that whatever you do, your kid is going to be messed up.

Please understand that this book is not addressed to you as a parent. It is addressed to you in that you were once a child. It is not so much about children's vulnerability to *bad* parenting as it is about their vulnerability to parenting, period. Children rarely articulate their faulty conclusions, and parents rarely guess them. No matter how hard you try, you cannot prevent your child from feeling helpless at times, nor can you anticipate every mistaken conclusion they may be drawing when they do.

To acknowledge your negative familiars and trace them to their source is not an indictment of your parents. *Everybody* has a painful childhood because being a child is inherently painful. It is a state of acute helplessness—

helplessness to control your world and helplessness to interpret it correctly. The result in adulthood is not that you are sick. It's that you are *stuck*. You are no longer helpless, yet you persist in habits of feeling that were originally born of helplessness. These habits stand in the way of fully enjoying adult life with the partner you have chosen.

In this book we will talk a lot about grieving. Indeed, you may begin to get the impression that "to grieve" is our favorite verb. We need to point out that the word has different connotations for us than it probably has for you. We view grieving as a very positive and life-affirming process. There is nothing depressing about it. In fact, grieving is the *opposite* of depression.

Grieving is how you get unstuck. It is how you move out of the unhappy past and into a healthy and promising present. To grieve is to revisit the old pain that gave rise to your negative familiars, acknowledge it, comfort it, and liberate yourself from its influence.

Whether you realize it or not, you have been carrying a burden of unacknowledged grief all your life. How do we know? Because we've never met anyone for whom this isn't true. It doesn't matter whether you consider your childhood happy or unhappy. Growing up is painful for *all* children. This pain is rarely acknowledged precisely because it is so universal. We tend to feel we have no right to feel sad about our childhood if nothing overtly terrible happened to us. The past sadness we don't give ourselves permission to feel seeps into the present, distorting our outlook on the world, our relationships, and our sense of self. A great many of the symptoms we're used to calling "stress-related" are actually grief-related.

The good news is that when you trace your unhappiness back to its original source, re-experience it, and comfort it, the present starts to look a whole lot happier. Childhood sorrow that is directly mourned begins to heal. Negative feelings you've always considered normal, because you've gotten so used to them, begin to dispel. You discover that you don't always have to feel that way. But, you may be wondering, what does all of this talk of childhood and grieving have to do with marriage?

When marriage becomes a drag—when you conceive of it as something you have to work on and can't seem to make any headway, no matter how hard you work—you are attempting to solve the wrong problem. If you are feeling unhappy in your marriage, then you are feeling unhappy, period. Individual pain is arising in the guise of relationship pain. Your partner can't do anything about your unhappiness, even if he tries. You feel failed by your partner because you are asking of him what it is not in his power to do. Both the source of your unhappiness and its remedy lie within yourself.

This may be a new idea to you, and we don't expect you to instantly agree with it. A great many marriage self-help books are premised on the idea that if your marriage is stale, stormy, or estranged, then the relationship itself is broken and something can and should be done to fix it. Couples who make a good faith effort to follow such advice without much result conclude that something must be wrong with themselves or their marriage, not with the advice. We hope to convince you otherwise by challenging the myths on which the advice is based. Our experience over twenty-five years of counseling has been that most people choose highly compatible partners and possess all of the inner resources they need to form affectionate, exciting, and deeply satisfying marriages. If they're struggling, it's usually because they are putting their efforts in the wrong place.

We don't work on our own relationship, much less anyone else's, because we know relationships can't be fixed and don't need to be fixed. Marriage feels painful when the old wounds of each partner are rubbed raw by contact with the other. The remedy is to not keep tinkering with the nature of that contact. The remedy is to heal the wound itself.

Most people have spent a lifetime denying their wounds. Breaking through this denial doesn't happen overnight. When they finally do, it will make them feel worse before it makes them feel better. But the payoffs are fantastic. People will discover that they don't have problems with intimacy after all. The hassles they thought they were having with their partners turn out to be hassles they were having with themselves. They discover that it's possible to satisfy and be satisfied by another person without bending each other out of shape. They finally get the power and control they've always longed for.

We will not go so far as to promise that the approach we're taking will save your marriage. A few of our clients have divorced, and we ourselves ended marriages of long standing before finding happiness with each other. Whether your own efforts to grow result in a better marriage with your current partner will depend to some extent on whether that person is making a reciprocal effort to grow. The gift you give yourself when you heal old wounds and expand your capacity for intimacy is yours to keep for life. Whether with your current partner or with another, you will discover the joy of love in the present tense.

Great relationships require **identical core values.** *reality*

Chapter 1

You'll actually hear two schools of thought on this. One maintains that shared interests and similarity of temperament comprise the recipe for lasting compatibility. After all, the reasoning goes, when the initial sexual thrill wears off, you'll be glad you have in common that passion for backgammon and *Star Trek* reruns. Conversely, if you're the pinstripe type, then your beloved's penchant for body piercing is going to seem a lot less cute once the honeymoon is over.

The other school of thought maintains that if you can get bored with sex, then you can certainly get bored with backgammon and *Star Trek* as well. A person who is just like you has nothing new to contribute to your life, whereas your opposite will continually challenge you and shake you out of your rut. No individual possesses the full inventory of desirable qualities in a human being, so the best plan is to marry the qualities you lack. The body-piercer saves the pinstriper from a life of dull conformity while the pinstriper saves the body-piercer from tetanus and *People*'s Worst Dressed List.

The debate has raged for as long as anyone can remember. It is never resolved because examples of successful marriages can be cited in support of both hypotheses. We're here to settle it once and for all by asserting that both sides have it wrong. Tastes, interests, temperaments, and personality types are simply irrelevant to the success or failure of marriages. In those areas, you may choose your opposite, your clone, or anything in between. Suit yourself. It doesn't matter.

What does matter is that you and your partner share identical core values. That's right: We said *identical.* The more closely your values match your partner's, the better your chances are of building a lasting, happy marriage. Any difference in your values is going to become a source of destructive conflict. Count on it. Even if you never argue about the value itself, believing you've simply agreed to disagree, the difference will surface in every quarrel you will have for the rest of your lives.

Values are the principles that guide our conduct in relation to other people. They express how we think we ought to behave toward others and how we think others ought to behave toward us. When we act out a value, we are doing our bit to make the world what we believe it *should be,* not necessarily what we believe it *is.* For example, many people cheat on their partners and get away with it. But if in your vision of an ideal world, spouses are truthful with one another, then you do not deceive your partner. That's a value, a principle that guides your actions regardless of whether you are happy about the potential consequences. In a constantly changing world, values serve as an anchor, a touchstone that we can always turn to when in doubt about what to do. They create the only clarity available to us in an ambiguous universe.

Values are black and white, all or nothing, and situation-neutral. If you really value honesty, then you tell the truth in *all* situations, not just when it's convenient. You can't imagine any realistic scenario in which you'd feel good about lying. If truthfulness is a value for you, then any lie you tell will cost you. Your self-esteem will be diminished by it, and so will your clarity about who you are. Compromising your values leads to a loss of faith in yourself and in the world. It leads to cynicism, depression, and, even sometimes, illness.

This is why married couples must agree on their core values about relationships, even if they disagree about everything else. People who live together usually make some compromises for the sake of domestic harmony. But values are the one aspect of a person that *cannot* be compromised—even slightly—without grievous injury to the integrity of the self. Compromise your values for your partner, and you lose yourself. Ultimately you are likely to lose the marriage as well. Marriage partners must therefore agree on their fundamental values because they will never be able to resolve a values conflict by splitting the difference. It is a given that if both partners are true to themselves, then the conflict will persist for as long as they are married.

Since values express our ideal of how relationships should be, a couple who shares values likewise shares a vision. Ask them to describe an ideal marriage, and they will paint nearly identical pictures. When two people are looking at the same "big picture," joint decision-making becomes easier. They agree on what outcome they want and have only to debate which alternative is mostly likely to lead to it. Having the same ideal in mind, they are more likely to achieve it. Shared values lead to shared goals.

Goals are specific things that you want to do, such as buying a house, taking an extended vacation, or starting a family. Unlike values, goals shift over time. You can change your mind about them or adjust them to accommodate your partner. Values are the ideals that influence your choice of goals. When you drop or change a goal, you do not change the underlying value.

Sometimes couples mistake shared goals for shared values. For instance, a couple might agree on the goal of attaining a certain income level. One partner values the pursuit of excellence in a meaningful career. She would want to work hard regardless of financial need and sees the income target merely as a measure of achievement. For the other it is seen as a means to an end—an early, secure retirement from a job that he finds meaningless. Although the goal is identical, the underlying values about work are actually the opposite. The clash of values will become painfully evident once the goal is attained. It is also likely to be expressed in conflicts about *how* to attain the goal. The partner who is pursuing security may pressure the one who values achievement to remain in a dead-end but lucrative job, compromising the very value that led her to set the income goal in the first place.

Values are the most permanent aspect of our character. Our tastes, interests, appearances, and even certain aspects of our personality all change over time. Core values don't. This might not seem obvious at first because many people change their religion, their political party, or their opinions about various issues. But all of these changes are themselves motivated by core values that go deeper than our opinions or affiliations. If you ask yourself *why* you changed your mind about an issue or dropped out of an organization to which you'd once felt loyal, you will begin to identify the core values underlying these decisions.

At the age when most people marry, they are not yet able to articulate their core values. They confuse values with opinions and, most especially, with parental "shoulds" and "oughts" internalized during childhood. As we mature, we throw off many of these internal shibboleths as our true values emerge. Nevertheless, our core values have been present all along even if, when we are young, we can't say what they are. Because they are permanent, values form the most reliable basis for a lasting marriage. The interests that you think you share with your partner at the time you get engaged will very likely change over time. Your shared values will not change.

Some Values Are Better Than Others

All values are not created equal. While shared values in general are essential if a marriage is to survive, we believe that certain values work better than others if you want your marriage to *thrive*.

Which values do we think work best? Our own, naturally.

Though few marriage counselors will admit this, all relationship advice is values-based. Anyone who tells you how to have a better relationship is operating out of some vision of what a better relationship looks like—in other words, a set of values. These value judgments are often masked by euphemisms such as "dysfunctional" or "inappropriate." Make no mistake: If a therapist tells you your relationship is dysfunctional, they mean that it is lousy. We once heard a therapist refer to a husband's habit of hitting on babysitters as "age-inappropriate behavior." You won't hear that kind of mealy-mouthing from us. We're judgmental, and we think you should be judgmental too.

Does this mean we're trying to impose our values on you? We couldn't if we tried. You're an adult, and your value system was already in place before you ever picked up this book. But we intend to state our values forthrightly at the outset so that you can get a clear picture of what we mean by "a great marriage." If you or your partner reject the values on which it is based, then our advice isn't going to work for you.

Our own marriage and our work with other couples are based on the following eight core values:

1. Personal Growth

A good marriage fosters personal growth, and personal growth fosters a good marriage. By growth we mean a continual process of learning about yourself, expanding your point of view, and extending yourself into the world.

People who are committed to personal growth are constantly asking themselves why they do what they do and feel what they feel. When confronted with setbacks, they are eager to explore what has gone wrong and how to do better next time. When they find themselves in conflict with others, they are interested in learning what the conflict has to teach them about themselves. They take risks and try out new behaviors. They don't consider themselves a finished product. They expect to keep changing right up to the moment they breathe their last breath.

We believe that the leading cause of failed marriages is failure on the part of one or both partners to grow. If your partner doesn't grow, then he becomes boring to you. If you don't grow, then you become boring to yourself.

Many people fear that if they grow, then they will grow apart from their partner. What people usually mean when they say "we grew apart" is that one partner changed and the other didn't. This rarely happens when growth itself is a shared value. If you value growth, you are interested in finding out *why* a change in your partner threatens or displeases you. The change in your partner becomes an impetus to your own growth. An individual's growth threatens a marriage only when her spouse clings to the status quo and refuses to examine his own reactions.

2. Willingness to Challenge Each Other

You care most for your partner when you demand that he become the best that he can be. In relationships where mutual challenge is a value, it is not acceptable for either partner to fall into a protracted slump. Each partner holds the other accountable for living up to his best vision of himself and for continuing to grow. Challenge is a vote of confidence, a sign of respect.

Conversely, accepting people exactly as they are is a form of abandonment. The message you send when you unconditionally accept a partner's self-destructive or self-defeating behavior is that you believe that she can't do better. Ultimately this defeats the marriage itself. In a mood of lazy tolerance, both partners grow increasingly hopeless and resigned, believing they are neither capable of attaining nor deserving of anything better. When you don't challenge your partner, you are essentially giving up on her.

3. Preeminence of the Adult Relationship

We believe that marriage works best when it is given a higher priority than any other relationship in either partner's life. All other relationships—including those with friends, family of origin, and your own children—come second. In our child-centered society this will sound to some like heresy. But putting each other first is actually one of the greatest gifts that you can give to your children.

Relationships with children are necessarily lacking in reciprocity. The adult gives more than the child can reasonably be expected to return. No child is capable of meeting an adult's needs for intimacy. The unmet needs of adults who neglect their marriages in an excessive focus on parenting become a terrible burden on their children. The children feel responsible for making their parents happy and end up blaming themselves for the deterioration of the adult relationship.

4. Dedication to Your Life's Purpose

Marriage is not your mission in life. Neither is raising children. You will never be satisfied with your relationship if you are expecting it to supply the fulfillment that comes from pursuing a vision. In a great marriage, each partner is deeply committed to and actively involved in some endeavor outside the marriage. Most often this is a person's career, but *what* you are dedicated to matters less than being dedicated to *something* that gives your life meaning and purpose, something that demands an all-out effort and the fullest expression of your talents and values.

When one partner is dedicated to an outside purpose while the other is dedicated only to supporting his spouse, then the supporting spouse ends up living through his partner in the same way unfulfilled parents live through their children. The one who is fully engaged with the outside world soon grows bored with her devoted supporter. Working only to "bring home the bacon" is likewise stultifying to a marriage. No matter how fat the paycheck is, you are not a full person or a full partner if your paycheck is all that you have to show at the end of the day.

5. Inner Renewal

Another word for this is "spirituality," but we'd like to avoid the religious connotations of that term. A shared religion is not essential to marriage. What is essential is that each partner regularly tap into some source of inner renewal. For some people this is accomplished through religious services or practices such as meditation, but it can also come from the enjoyment of nature or art, exercise or hobbies, journaling, or simply spending quiet time alone with oneself.

Whatever your source of inner renewal, its value to a marriage is the strength it brings to each partner as an individual. When you care for yourself in this way, you stay in touch with your own inner life, replenish your energy, put everyday hassles into perspective, and gain the strength to pull through crises. Without the regular practice of inner renewal, it is very difficult, perhaps impossible, to actualize any of the other values that make for great marriages.

6. Personal Responsibility

As a shared value, personal responsibility is an agreement in principle about what marriage partners are—and are not—responsible *for*. In a great marriage, both partners assume full responsibility for their own inner lives. This means that you don't view your partner as the cause of what you are feeling. Nor do you view yourself as the cause of what he is feeling. You don't blame your partner for your own unhappiness, nor do you blame yourself for his. It is mutually understood that while you can't control what your partner does, you are completely free to choose your own *response* to what he does.

7. Accountability

Accountability is the flip side of personal responsibility. While we are not responsible for our spouse's feelings, we are accountable for our actions and the impact of those actions on our relationship. Accountability in marriage means keeping one's word, following through on commitments, telling the truth, and accepting the full consequences of what we do and neglect to do. In a great marriage, spouses hold both themselves and their partners accountable. Just as it is a failure of accountability to lie to your partner, it is likewise a failure of accountability not to confront the lies that are told to you.

8. Quality Communication

In a relationship where individual growth and dedication to purposes outside the marriage are held as values, it is essential to stay current with each other. Often spouses imagine that their marriage lacks intimacy because they don't spend enough time together. Believing this, they may become resentful of their partners' outside interests. Real intimacy is based on the *quality* of communication. This means regularly sharing with your partner what's happening in your inner life and listening with full attention when your partner shares with you.

Sounds Good on Paper, But. . . .

As you read over our list of core values, you may find yourself readily agreeing with them in the abstract. Few people would say that they are *against* personal growth, accountability, or communication. But these principles cannot properly be considered your values unless they influence your everyday actions. If an idea is truly a value for you, then it forms the basis for your decisions. You choose it even when it is in conflict with your immediate desires and even when you experience outside pressure to abandon it. For a true value, you are willing to pay a price.

The following questions are designed to help you reflect on the extent to which our eight core values currently influence your actions and the extent to which they would influence your decisions in difficult predicaments. We recommend that you and your spouse work through these questions alone at first, writing down your answers. Next, set aside a couple of hours to share your responses with each other and discuss them.

Value #1: Personal Growth

1. Over the past year, what have you worked hardest to change or develop in yourself? Of what recent personal growth achievement are you most proud?
2. In what ways have you seen your partner grow over the past year? For what personal growth achievement do you especially admire your partner?
3. Your partner is offered an attractive new job in another state. Because you are self-employed and work from home, the move will not hurt your own career, so you readily agree to it. But after the move, you feel unhappy. Your partner enjoys plenty of social contact at work while you feel isolated in your home office and are slower to make new friends. Your partner

complains that you have suddenly become clingy and demanding. What do you do?

Value #2: Willingness to Challenge

1. Your partner, who used to be very outgoing and active, has lately turned into a couch potato. She spends most evenings in a stupor, snacking and channel-surfing and has begun to put on a lot of weight. What do you do?
2. You are having a lot of trouble getting along with your new boss. Many evenings you come home and relate to your partner stories about what a jerk this person is. After a couple of weeks of this, your partner suggests to you that your own hostility may be contributing to your problems at work. How do you react?
3. When you decide not to confront your partner about a difficult issue, what reason do you give yourself for your refusal to challenge?

Value #3: Preeminence of the Adult Relationship

1. Do you feel like you are #1 in your partner's life? If not, who do you believe comes before you?
2. You and your partner have a standing date to spend "alone time" together one evening a week. Your two-year-old stages a predictable temper tantrum every week just as the babysitter arrives. You believe that your child is suffering separation anxiety on these occasions, and you feel guilty about going out. What do you do?

3. On several occasions, you have overheard your spouse gossiping to his or her best friend about you, revealing intimate details of your relationship that you would prefer to keep private. When you tell your partner how you feel about this, your partner replies that best friends tell each other everything and that what goes on in the relationship with the friend is none of your business. How do you respond?

Value #4: Dedication to Your Life's Purpose

1. You are making a lot of money at a job that no longer challenges or fulfills you. You are offered an exciting new opportunity with a company that is just starting up. While accepting the new position will afford you exactly the type of challenge you need to grow professionally, it will also entail a substantial cut in pay and the risk that you or the new company could fail. If you take the new job, it will not be possible to buy the vacation home on which you and your partner had set your hearts. What do you do?

2. Your partner is suddenly gaining national recognition for her endeavors: being interviewed by the press, speaking at conventions, and so forth, and traveling two or three days out of every week. While you are proud of your partner, you are also feeling neglected and envious of all the attention she is receiving. What do you do?

Value #5: Inner Renewal

1. What practices or activities give you a sense of inner renewal? Of these activities, which is the most important to you?
2. When was the last time that you did the activity that you selected as most important?
3. When you're feeling completely drained, what do you do to recharge your batteries?

Value #6: Personal Responsibility

1. You have an opportunity to travel abroad for six weeks in pursuit of your most passionate interest. It will not be possible for your partner to accompany you, and, deep down, you find the idea of taking the trip alone rather exciting. Your partner is upset at the prospect of such a long separation and keeps expressing the irrational fear that you will be unfaithful while you are away. What do you do?
2. Now switch places and imagine that it is your partner who has the opportunity to travel abroad and you who feel afraid that she will be unfaithful. What do you do?
3. Your partner takes the risk of confiding a secret sexual fantasy that he would like the two of you to act out together. The fantasy doesn't appeal to you at all—in fact, it makes you rather squeamish. Your partner complains that your inhibitions are the cause of his sexual boredom and frustration. How do you respond?

Value #7: Accountability

1. On the opening day of baseball season, your partner calls in sick and goes to the game. You are at home when your partner's boss calls with an urgent question. Do you admit that your partner is not at home, or do you say that she is too sick to come to the phone?

2. You and your partner maintain separate credit card accounts. You have agreed that each of you will pay your personal debts out of your own earnings and that you don't have to consult each other before making charges to these private accounts. When you are laid off from your job, your partner, who could easily afford to take over your credit card payments, refuses to do so. Do you think that this is justified?

3. Your partner has agreed to be home by 6 p.m. to stay with the kids while you go out to dinner with a friend. Detained by a minor crisis at work, your partner gets home at 7:30 p.m. As it turns out, your dinner engagement was cancelled at the last minute, so his absence didn't actually cause a problem. What, if anything, do you say about it?

Value #8: Quality Communication

1. At the end of every day, your partner presents you with a litany of complaints about the world. You find this negativity a downer and have begun to tune your partner out, responding only with a bland "uh-huh"

every few minutes. Not surprisingly, your partner accuses you of not really listening. What should you do?

2. You and your partner had a lot of difficulty conceiving your first child, and when it finally happened, you were both ecstatic. Now, several months into the pregnancy, you are beginning to have misgivings. You feel anxious about the huge responsibility you've taken on and dismayed over the impending loss of freedom. Your spouse seems as happy as ever. Do you share your feelings?

As you will have discovered by working with them, these questions oblige you to consider not only the standards to which you hold yourself but also those to which you hold your partner. You might discover some inconsistencies. For example, you might have expressed a willingness to lie to cover for your partner even though you would never put her in the position of having to lie for you. Holding yourself to a higher standard implies a subtle disrespect for your partner. Holding yourself to a lower standard implies disrespect for yourself. Where such disparities exist, one partner tends to occupy a "one-up" position, indulging his partner's weaknesses while at the same time claiming the moral high ground.

When you and your partner compare answers, you might discover a pronounced clash around one or more of the values. It may become clear that when push comes to shove, one of you holds firmly to the principle that marriage partners should place each other first while the other is willing, in some circumstance, to let other relationships take priority. Does this mean that you have discovered a serious incompatibility? It might. In this clash of values, you may have identified the root cause of many of your quarrels. If there is indeed a conflict in deeply held values, then you are not going to be able to resolve it through compromise.

But don't panic. Initially it can be difficult to distinguish your true values from your familiar emotional reactions. For example, your child's tantrums may be triggering abandonment feelings carried over from your own childhood. The intensity of your reaction makes it difficult for you to bring your values into focus. Learning to separate such reactions from our true values will be a recurring theme of this book. By the time you've worked your way through the book, you will likely find that your values are emerging more clearly.

Our experience has been that most couples who go through values clarification together are pleasantly surprised to discover the extent to which they agree. While few people have consciously articulated their values at the time they choose a partner, on an unconscious level they gravitate to someone whose values are highly compatible. This is good news. When common values are identified and made explicit, couples discover a firm common ground from which they can work to resolve many conflicts that had previously seemed irresolvable. They discover that despite whatever dissatisfactions may be ruffling the surface of their marriage, they have chosen the right partner.

myth

Love will carry you
through the hard times
in a relationship.

It is **shared values**
that pull you
through a crisis.

reality

Chapter 2

24

The aptly titled film *What's Love Got to Do with It?*
follows Tina Turner through years of harrowing abuse by
her husband. He beats her, belittles her, humiliates her in
public, and literally drags her out of her hospital bed to
keep a concert engagement when she becomes gravely ill.
When friends, fearing for her very life, urge her to leave
him, she replies that she can't leave. She loves him.

Going to such extremes for love might seem crazy to
you, but on a mundane level, many people live by the
same mythology that motivated Tina Turner during that
period of her life. Tune in to any radio station at random,
and you'll hear it being sung. "Love will keep us
together." "Love will see us through." "Love is all you
need." Raised on the mythology that love is the medicine
that cures all relationship ills, most of us do our level best
to make it true. If our marriage is unhappy, then our first
idea of what to do about it is to love harder.

What, exactly, this all-conquering power actually
consists of is never quite defined, but pain would seem to
be one of its distinguishing features. Some people
experience it as a mysterious force of attraction that
prevents escape from a relationship even when it has
become all but intolerable. ("I'd rather be blue over you
than happy with anyone else.") Yet the eventual waning of
the attraction does not necessarily set its victims free. Love
then becomes redefined as a whole cluster of values—
commitment, endurance, forgiveness, tolerance—that
elevate to a virtue the perceived necessity of sticking with

someone who *doesn't* attract you. Love is what you tell yourself you're doing when you resign yourself to being perpetually disappointed and bored.

Do we—Morrie and Arleah—love each other? You bet we do. But if you ask us what makes our marriage happy, you won't hear talk of love. A word so constantly applied to wooly-minded self-abandonment communicates nothing meaningful about what makes good relationships tick. As Tina Turner sanely concluded, "What's love got to do with it?"

Why You Love the One Who Hurts You

When we first met Greta, she was on the brink of divorcing Dave, her husband of six years. "He's so domineering, I feel I can hardly breathe," she said. She followed this up with an inventory of Dave's controlling behaviors: demanding that she drop everything the moment he wanted her attention; throwing jealous fits; monopolizing every conversation; and flying into a rage if she declined his sexual initiatives. What she meant was immediately evident when we saw them together. Dave interrupted her constantly. When he let her complete a statement at all, he immediately rephrased it. He'd begin, "What Greta means to say is. . . ." and follow that up with something she hadn't meant to say at all. Each time this happened, Greta looked sulky but did not protest.

When asked why she had been putting up with this for six years, Greta responded predictably that she loved Dave. "I actually did leave once for a couple of months. But the whole time we were separated, I pined away for him. One evening we got together to discuss a legal separation, and within twenty minutes we were hitting the sheets. I can't help it. I think of leaving all the time, but the love is too strong. I can't really imagine life without him."

We asked Greta whether the feeling of being overwhelmed by another person was familiar for her. She hesitated a moment. "Sort of. Dave is nothing like my mother, but in a different way, I guess you could say I felt overwhelmed by her. When I was a kid, she was into the whole child beauty pageant scene. A real stage mother. Everything had to be perfect, down to my little toenails. Dave's not fussy like that. But now that you mention it, the way I feel around both of them is pretty much the same. Maybe there's something in me that subconsciously longs to be dominated. Is that where you're going with this?"

No, we were not going to say that. Greta was attracted to Dave not because she liked his dominating behavior but because the feelings it evoked in her were so familiar. Around Dave she didn't feel happy, yet she felt like *herself*. She couldn't imagine life without him because she couldn't imagine feeling any other way.

There is in every intimate relationship a strong pull from the past. We are attracted to people who evoke in us our most ancient feeling states, who make us feel the way we did when we were children. Some of these feelings are negative because being a child is hard. As kids, we felt helpless. We *were* helpless. We knew that we would not survive if our parents abandoned us. Along with our passionate attachment to them, we felt anxious, uncertain of how to control these inscrutable, powerful adults on whom our lives depended. Every child comes up with some instinctive strategy to manage his helplessness, and all of us are wounded to some degree by what we did to manage.

Feelings that have been with us since childhood are our *familiars*. They are the emotional patterns that we tend to fall into as adults, even though we are no longer living with the outward circumstances that first provoked them. Although we may have learned to *behave* differently as adults, we go on *feeling* the way we felt as children. When these feelings are triggered by something happening in the present, they seem perfectly natural to us. We have difficulty even imagining that there might be any other way to feel. Familiars—even when they are unpleasant—make us feel safe. We might not like what's happening, but at least we know what to expect.

When Greta performed poorly in child beauty pageants, her mother had become cold and withdrawn in her disappointment. As adults we may understand that another adult's disappointment is her own responsibility and that we are not to blame for it. Children do not understand this. Greta experienced her mother's coldness as abandonment and assumed—as children always assume—that it was her own fault. While preparing for pageants, though, her mother lavished time and attention on her. Most of this attention took the form of fussing and nitpicking. It wasn't exactly pleasant, but at least it wasn't abandonment. Although Greta can't remember any incident from childhood that was particularly traumatic, what she remembers feeling on an everyday basis was a kind of dull passivity as she submitted to the many demands of her perfectionist mother. That is her *familiar*—the feeling state that seems most characteristic of her simply because she felt that way so often.

When they first married, Greta congratulated herself on finding a partner who was the opposite of her mother. Where her mother used to turn frosty and distant when displeased, Dave got bombastic. He was loud but communicative. To Greta, this seemed like an improvement. His tantrums felt less like abandonment to her than her mother's withdrawal. Yet she found herself appeasing Dave in his hot rages the same way she used to appease her mother's cold sulks. She lapsed immediately into the feeling of morose passivity that was her familiar.

It might not be immediately obvious that Dave, who has adopted the role of bully, has also found a partner who evokes his familiar. His busy parents had overindulged his whims. When he threw tantrums, they found it expedient to give him whatever he asked for. They failed to offer what he didn't know how to ask for—a sense of limits. For a child, it is frightening not to know where the limits are. Disliked by other children for his overbearing ways, Dave did not know how to behave differently. He concluded that he was just not a very nice person and resigned himself to the idea that he would always be rejected by others. While Greta grew up fearing that she would be abandoned by her mother if she didn't win beauty pageants, Dave grew up feeling abandoned, period. Greta, in her reluctance to put her foot down when Dave bullies her, evokes in him the familiar childhood feeling of being out of control. When she sulks or cries and accuses him of being a tyrant, he feels like the person he has always felt himself to be. He *expects* to feel isolated and rejected and to believe it is his own fault. It is painful yet irresistibly attractive in its very familiarity.

Like most couples, Greta and Dave are attracted to the pain they feel when they are together. Why? Because it's predictable. If given a choice between unfamiliar pleasure and pain we've grown used to, most of us will choose the latter. The familiar gives us a sense of security. Excuse us if we sound unromantic, but the mysterious, irrational, and delicious pangs of love that have inspired so many songs come down to this one universal and not very mysterious reality. When you find someone who makes you feel lousy in exactly the way you felt lousy as a child, you believe that you are made for each other.

That might sound dismal, but upon this seemingly shaky foundation, truly great relationships can be built. In choosing our partners, we are attracted not only by the familiarity of the pain but also by the potential to grow beyond it. Greta did not choose Greg because she wanted to duplicate her relationship with her mother. Quite the contrary. She is attempting to outgrow her familiar by creating a different and better relationship with a partner who evokes the same feeling.

Greta and Dave made no mistake in marrying each other. They are a good match. What each of them needs to do to improve the marriage is precisely the thing that they need to do to grow as an individual. Greta, if she learns to stand up to Dave, will be setting the limits that he has always needed. Dave, if he begins to curb his impulses to control Greta, will challenge her to overcome her passivity. The person we have so unerringly chosen based on the allure of the familiar more often than not turns out to be exactly the *right* person for us—if (and this is a big IF) we are committed to personal growth.

How Values Help You Break the Grip of the Past

When we feel stuck in our relationships, locked into some problem or conflict that resists solution no matter what we do, we are experiencing a blast from the past. The crisis that brings a marriage to the brink of breakup was set in motion years before a couple met. It is rooted in their familiars.

You can't overcome the pull of the past unless there is an equally strong pull toward the present. This pull is provided by your shared vision and values. While your familiar expresses your (often negative) childhood conclusions about how the world really is, your values express what you think the world ought to be and what you *want* it to be. Without ever giving the matter much conscious thought, most people choose partners whose familiars *and* values are a good fit. Although the familiar is the aspect of your attraction that is rooted in the past, shared values form the basis of your attraction in the present and the foundation of your mutual respect. When shared values are put into action, they give you and your partner the forward momentum to overcome the drag of the familiar.

Although locked into a pattern of relating dictated by their familiars, neither Greta nor Dave was *satisfied* with this pattern. The very fact that they sought counseling demonstrates that they could conceive of and desire something better. Their mental pictures of what something better would look like were remarkably similar.

"I get envious when I hear another woman refer to her husband as 'my best friend,'" Greta confided. "That's how I want to feel about Dave. I want the kind of relationship where you tell each other everything, where there's no one you'd rather talk to than your partner."

"But you don't treat me like your best friend," Dave complained. "You treat me like an ogre."

"I know. I'm just saying how I *wish* it was."

"I wish it was like that, too. I wish you didn't clam up on me. You weren't always so wimpy. Remember?"

He went on to describe their second date, for which he'd shown up ninety minutes late. Habitual lateness was part of the pattern of controlling behavior that had sabotaged his previous relationships. His girlfriends complained and sulked but tolerated it until it became intolerable. Then, they dumped him. Greta's response was neither to tolerate Dave's rudeness nor to reject him. When he arrived to pick her up, he found her in her pajamas. "Tonight's off, I'm afraid," she said pleasantly. "I figured I'd been stood up, so I ordered a pizza and got into watching a video. Shall we make it another night?"

"That fascinated me," Dave recalled. "Greta refused to be jerked around. She was so friendly about the whole thing, yet she let me know that I'd better show up on time if I expected to take her out. That's when I first started falling for her. But once we were involved . . . I don't know; she just wimped out on me."

"It's true, I did," Greta admitted. "I don't know where I found the gumption to do what I did that night. I guess it's because I wasn't attached yet. At that point, I could take Dave or leave him. Once I got attached . . . I couldn't put my foot down anymore. Can't even *find* my feet most of the time."

"I liked you better the way you were that night," Dave admitted.

"I liked me better then, too."

What Greta and Dave mutually value is implicit in their nostalgia over this incident. She had been able to assert her limits without rejecting him because she took responsibility for her own happiness. She wasn't about to let an inconsiderate date spoil her evening. He respected her for this because personal responsibility is a value for him too. Both could agree that their marriage would be better if this value were more often applied to it. Both also shared a vision of a marriage in which they'd feel like best friends. They weren't sure how to achieve quality communication, but they could agree that it was a value on which they wanted to build their partnership.

"Look, Greta, if you'll agree to talk more, I'll try to stop interrupting you so much," Dave proposed.

"I'll try to talk more, if you'll stop interrupting," she countered.

The problem with these proposals was the "ifs." Although both could agree that their communication would be better if Greta were doing more of the talking, she would say that she was holding back because he was monopolizing the conversation while he would say that he was monopolizing the conversation because she was holding back. That's where they were getting stuck. As long as each person believes that her own behavior is being caused by her partner's, then nothing can change.

You just go around in circles, each waiting for the other to do something different.

While a couple may agree that a value is mutual, the decision to act on a value is individual. If something is truly a value for you, then you act on it *regardless* of what your partner is doing. To change the negative pattern, Dave would need to stop interrupting Greta, regardless of whether she was making an effort to talk more. And she would need to make that effort, regardless of whether Dave was interrupting. Such unilateral initiatives are scary. To change without any guarantee that your partner will change means facing the very discomfort that you've been trying to avoid with your old patterns.

At our next session, Dave reported that he was making a conscious effort to stop himself from interrupting. He was thrilled to discover his own capacity to grow. "I've always been a blowhard," he admitted. "Always felt that was beyond my control, that it was just the way I am. I'm amazed to find that I *can* control myself, once I set my mind to it. I think I'm becoming less of a jerk."

Greta agreed. "Yeah, I'm amazed, too. I never imagined Dave would knock himself out like this to do something I asked. He's really worked hard at it. Only. . . . " she hesitated, casting an apologetic glance at her husband.

"Only?"

"Only the trouble is, I still don't feel we're really communicating," Greta admitted. "I mean, now I've got the floor, but for some reason I don't feel like I'm getting my point across. Once I've got his attention, I feel like I don't even know anymore what I wanted to say. It just sort of fades away. I guess I still don't believe Dave really *wants* to listen to me."

"I do!" Dave bellowed. "I'm giving you my undivided attention whenever you open your mouth. What more proof do you need?"

At his raised voice, Greta shrank. "I don't know," she said morosely. "Maybe, I really *don't* have anything to say. That's how you make me feel. Like what I'm thinking isn't really important. I can't explain what you're doing to make me feel like that. I only know it's how I feel."

Dave isn't making Greta feel discounted. Her familiar is making her feel that way. When what she intends to say "just fades away," she is experiencing the pull of her old patterns, the passivity with which she has been resigning herself to ever since she was a child. That habitual feeling is so strong that it obscures the fact that Dave is actually sitting there expectantly and ready to hang on her every word. She can't believe he's really interested because she's not used to believing that she might be interesting.

Although Greta's timidity is coming from the past, she is feeling it intensely in the present. To attribute it to Dave seems natural. After all, he's there, and her mother is not. However, when he makes the effort to listen better, she feels even more intimidated. Illogical as it may sound, to feel worse when our partner changes for the better is not uncommon. We are losing the security, the comfortable predictability of the old mutual pattern while still feeling the pull of our individual familiar. It feels a bit like being stranded on the dance floor in the middle of a very old song. Till then, you'd thought it was "our song." Now, you realize that you learned that song when you were very young, that it's been the theme song of your whole life. When your partner changes, you're left there dancing to it all by yourself.

Greta was offhand the first time she told us about her mother. This time she wept. Without Dave's bullying to focus on in the present, she felt her past pain more vividly. She recalled becoming tongue-tied on a pageant stage, forgetting all the cute things that her mother had coached her to say, then blurting out words of her own choosing. She remembered her mother's icy silence on the long drive home. "I truly thought it was Dave making me feel this way," she said as she dabbed at her ruined mascara. "But it isn't. I've *always* felt like this."

Dave, who'd been uncharacteristically subdued as she told her story, finally spoke up. "I never knew before what those pageants were like for you. When you've talked about it before, you were always so jokey."

"Yeah. Cute. Just like they taught me to be."

Seeing how much it hurt his partner to be discounted, Dave was even more determined to curb his overbearing ways. That doesn't mean that he was transformed overnight. He continued to engage in many of the behaviors that Greta had complained of during their first session with us. But now she was beginning to question the assumption that her lack of self-confidence was being caused by her husband. The more she saw the connection between her present feelings and the past, the less she felt overwhelmed by Dave. At our next session, she had a triumph to report.

"One night last week, Dave was pestering me to come to bed. I wanted to stay up and read. So he starts ranting as usual about how tense he is, what a hard day he's had at work—"

"Well, it *was* a hard day!"

"—how he won't be able to get to sleep unless I help him relax, how if he's wasted the next day, it will be all my fault. What gal could resist a come-on like that?" she quipped, and Dave had the grace to chuckle.

"Usually I just give in," Greta continued. "I figure okay, let's just get it over with—"

"And what guy could resist an attitude like that?" Dave put in.

"Touché!" Greta said, laughing. "Anyway, this time I just went on sitting there with my book. I said, 'So you're tense, poor dear. Who's problem is that?'"

"Yours, baby," Dave jested.

"In your dreams, baby," Greta shot back.

They both laughed. We asked Dave how he'd felt about this incident.

"Horny," he said. "Greta's not letting me push her around is a turn-on. But as she has now informed me in no uncertain terms, that's my problem." He grinned at her, and she smiled fondly back. We had the impression that, but for our presence, she would have been amenable to solving his "problem" on the spot.

We noticed that Dave had interrupted Greta twice during this exchange. We also noticed that Greta herself appeared not to have noticed. Unfazed, she just went right on telling her story. As she learned to take responsibility for her own familiar, she began to discover new options. Instead of always pressing Dave to change, she could change her own response to his behavior. She could cut him some slack about his tendency to interrupt because it no longer intimidated her. This is quite the opposite of the resignation to a partner's faults that usually goes by the name of "love." It is because she is *not* resigned that the occasional lapse has become easier to take in stride. A single interruption no longer makes her feel doomed to a lifetime of feeling overwhelmed.

How Values Simplify Difficult Decisions

Soon after we married, we faced financial difficulties. It was the second marriage for both of us, and we had children from our previous marriages to support. We were both in the middle of career changes, and we were also deeply in debt. "Looks like we're going to have to tighten our belts and put ourselves on a strict budget," Arleah observed with a sigh. She said this with the air of someone stating the obvious.

Morrie gaped at her in utter disbelief. "That's the most preposterous idea I've ever heard!"

Arleah comes from a poor family in rural Indiana. She was raised to believe that when funds are short, you simply do without. Debt makes her nervous. Morrie comes from an affluent Jewish family on Chicago's North Shore. He was raised to believe that if you don't have enough money, you go out and make more. Our debt level would have to approach the federal budget deficit before he lost any sleep over it.

Sounds like a pretty major area of incompatibility, doesn't it? Money is high on the list of topics that couples fight about, so you are probably expecting us to confess that our wildly differing attitudes about money have been a constant source of strife. In fact, we don't fight about it at all.

What's our secret? Values. We agreed early on that financial decisions would not be based on our familiars. Neither Arleah's native caution nor Morrie's munificence would dictate how we managed our money. Instead, we would consult our values and our shared vision of how we wanted to live.

About ten years into our marriage, we realized that we were no longer happy living in the suburbs of Chicago. We wanted to move but did not, at first, know *where* we wanted to move. Based on our shared values, we developed a list of criteria. A love of the outdoors is a major source of inner renewal for both of us, so we wanted our new home to be situated on a large tract of wilderness land. Since our commitment to our work leads us to travel constantly, we needed to live within easy reach of an airport. We also wanted our home itself to be a great place to work. We wanted to live in an area where people shared our work ethic and in a state where the political life reflects our own political views. As we developed our mutual vision, our list eventually grew to about twenty firm requirements. We wondered if we would ever be able to identify a place that satisfied all of them. It took about three years of searching, but eventually we found a property that was *everything* we wanted.

Buying our land and building our dream house entailed a huge investment. This goal shaped all of our financial decisions from the time we first conceived of it until the time it was achieved. Once we began to design the house, there were hundreds of choices to be made, and each of these choices was based on our shared values. At one point, the contractor cautioned us that the design we'd proposed had a ridiculous number of windows. Our heating and cooling bills could be staggering. We were daunted for a minute or two. But then we consulted our motivating value—inner renewal through contact with nature. We agreed that those windows were essential to our satisfaction.

Because our decisions were driven by a shared vision, we experienced very little conflict over them. That doesn't mean that the process was easy. Arleah frequently had to wrestle with her instinctive reluctance to spend, the familiar arising from her penny-pinching childhood. When anxiety arose, she shared it, and we explored it together. But values, not familiars, motivated our decisions. As a result of rising to this challenge, Arleah now lives in the house of her dreams. Although she will probably never be as relaxed about spending as Morrie is, she has gradually come to enjoy it. She has learned that she doesn't have to be limited by the attitudes ingrained in her as a child.

All areas of potential conflict in marriage—from child-rearing to sex to who takes out the garbage—can be approached the way we approach our finances. Quarrels in these areas typically boil down to a competition between his familiar and her familiar. Regardless of who wins such a contest, *neither* partner will truly be satisfied. Familiars drive you to seek what you needed as a child, not what you need today. Happiness based on the fulfillment of these obsolete needs will forever elude you. They arise from a past that can never be made happier, no matter what you do in the present.

Values bring you back to the present where, as an adult, you are fully capable of attaining what you want and need *now*. In a values-based decision, both partners can win big. Provided the motivating value is fully shared, both partners will get what they want. That is because what you *truly* want is to be found in your values, not in your familiars.

So, What's Love Got to Do with It?

You are drawn to your partner by compatible familiars as well as compatible values. Your attraction is a complex mixture of impulses: to heal the past and to remain stuck in it, to seize the challenge of the present and to conspire together to avoid it. The love that you feel for your partner expresses both your highest ideals and your deepest wounds. Sometimes your partner is a salve on your wound. Sometimes he is salt in it.

Love is a many-splendored thing, but it is not a solution. When a marriage gets mired in destructive patterns rooted in the distant past, it is shared values that move you forward into a happier present. Values do not obliterate the pain of the past, but they enable you to make new and better choices. The more you can acknowledge the influence of your past on how you feel in the present, the freer you become to act in accordance with your values. When these values are shared and acted upon in your marriage, you feel attracted to your partner for all the best reasons. You respect, admire, and *enjoy* her, and you respect yourself for loving her.

myth *You **need to work** on your marriage if you want it to be good.*

*Relationships don't have problems; **people do.*** **reality**

Chapter 3

Our relationship has so far proven impervious to destruction by external forces, ranging from the mildly stressful to the catastrophic. We've built two houses of our own design without ever getting into a serious fight over it. We've weathered frequent separations due to the demands of our respective careers and faced the challenge of step-parenting adolescent children from previous marriages. We've coped with money troubles, a major relocation, the death of a child, and a battle with cancer. Our marriage has come out of each of these crises stronger than ever. Nevertheless, we did, on one occasion, approach the brink of divorce.

What was the issue that nearly proved our undoing?

Chicken soup.

The conflict that was ultimately to become The Great Chicken Soup Fight had been on a slow simmer for nearly a decade—such a slow simmer that it had never given off any noticeable steam.

Morrie's high housekeeping standards had, early in our marriage, led him to establish a Ten-Point Checklist of Kitchen Cleanliness. Since he was frequently away on business, the actual execution of the Ten-Point Checklist usually fell to Arleah. Many women of Arleah's professional stature might have taken exception to this demand, but Arleah, who values the pursuit of excellence in all things, chose to adopt Morrie's standards as a spur to domestic greatness.

Whenever Morrie returned from a business trip, his first act was to conduct a reconnaissance of the kitchen.

He could not unpack or unwind without first inspecting every surface, fixture, and appliance to determine whether it was in Ten-Point compliance. Irregularities such as crumbs in the toaster tray or a wet dishrag left in the sink were brought to Arleah's immediate attention. On average, she managed to comply with eight points out of ten. On the night of the Great Chicken Soup Fight, however, she had at last achieved compliance with all ten points.

Was Morrie happy? He was not. Turning to face Arleah from the open refrigerator, he barked, *"There's no chicken soup!"*

For ten years Arleah had been taking Morrie's homecoming ritual in stride. It truly hadn't bothered her. She could see the funny side of it. Now, quite suddenly, it bothered her big time. She'd had it up to here with the Ten Points of Kitchen Cleanliness. She asserted, furthermore, that she was not put on this earth to cater to Morrie's chicken soup fetish. When Morrie obstinately refused to acknowledge the merits of this position, she got in her car and drove away. She told him that she was leaving for good. At that moment, she really meant it.

Maybe you've had silly fights like this. You start out arguing about a bank overdraft or underwear left on the floor, and, before you know it, tears are being shed, walls are being punched, and divorce is being threatened. When that happens, your fight has nothing to do with the present. Problems arising in the present are readily solved in the present. If there's no chicken soup in the house, you do without or go buy some. What's the big deal? The big deal for Morrie had nothing to do with Arleah or our marriage, much less his hunger for soup. The emotion that fueled the quarrel was coming from the distant past.

Morrie grew up in a houseful of women who were incessantly occupied with cooking and cleaning. When he came home from school, they listened absently to his tales of triumph and woe, responding not with words or hugs but with snacks and freshly laundered clothes. Love was expressed through domestic exertion. If you came home to chicken soup and a kitchen so clean that you could perform open-heart surgery on the counters, then you were to conclude that you were cared for.

For years, Morrie had been demanding that Arleah express caring in the way that he was used to receiving it, and Arleah had been doing her best to accommodate him. But eight out of Ten Points of Kitchen Cleanliness couldn't make him happy. Even *ten* out of Ten Points of Kitchen Cleanliness couldn't make him happy. When Arleah finally succeeded in meeting every one of his housekeeping demands, he felt empty. He felt like something was still missing. That something had always been missing for Morrie. In the kitchen Arleah had made spotless to please him, he was at last faced with the realization that spotlessness had never hit the spot for him. What emerged that night in the guise of anger with Arleah was the disappointment he'd so often felt as a child.

No matter what she did, Arleah couldn't win. She was willing to give him what he'd asked for—an impeccably clean kitchen. She was also willing to give him what he truly needed when he came home from a trip—attention, affection, and interest. But Morrie could not at that moment be satisfied with *anything* that Arleah did because what was bugging him had been bugging him for years before he even met her. It wasn't her problem. It wasn't our marriage's problem. It was, quite simply, Morrie's problem.

Couples often worry that their relationship is in trouble when they find themselves falling again and again into highly emotional conflicts that resist resolution. Triggered by something seemingly trivial, these fights have a way of escalating very quickly to the "You don't really love me" stage. When a hassle over the kitchen sink blows up into conflagration about everything *but* the kitchen sink, couples tend to assume that it is symptomatic of deep-seated, unresolved issues in their relationship. They conclude that the relationship needs work.

What people usually mean when they say, "We need to work on our relationship," is that they feel bad and want the other person to change so that they can feel better. The one who feels the relationship needs to be worked on typically initiates a long talk. Earnestly, she explains to her partner what a schmuck he is, why this bothers her, and what he should do in order to render himself less schmuck-like. If he challenges the proposition that he is a schmuck, then the conversation derails into a fight over his perception of reality versus her perception of reality. After many repetitions of this fruitless discussion, the couple may visit a counselor. The counselor is viewed as an impartial judge before whom each argues his or her version of reality in hopes that the judge will agree with his or her side and tell his or her partner to change.

If a counselor willingly assumes this role during the first session, don't waste your money on further sessions. That counselor is as mixed up about relationships as you are. The basic premise that one adult's feelings can be caused by another adult is faulty, and nothing can come of it but further pointless conflict and confusion.

Emotional pain in a relationship comes about when the relationship triggers our familiars-emotions rooted in the distant past. Familiars may complicate relationships, but they are not caused by the relationship itself, nor can they be helped by it. There is nothing your partner can do about how you felt as a child. The fact that you're now feeling this way all over again around your partner does not necessarily mean that your partner is doing something wrong or that anything is wrong with your marriage. Your pain is a signal that you yourself need to grow.

The Contrast Place

One couple we know, Kate and Stan, literally do fight about the kitchen sink. The plumbing in their house is old and prone to malfunction. When a sink plugs up or leaks, Stan spends a day taking it apart and putting it back together again. This would be a rational response if Stan possessed plumbing skills. He does not. The usual result of his exertions is that a minor drip becomes Niagara Falls. When Kate sensibly observes that the services of a professional plumber would be of benefit, Stan flies into a rage. Exasperated by his stubbornness and the flood on the kitchen floor, Kate yells back.

Stan comes from a large blue-collar family that values practical skills more highly than intellectual achievement, especially in males. He is the eldest of ten children and the only one to have earned a college degree. Throughout his childhood, he was teased for his bookishness, made to feel like something of a freak. His seven brothers all went into practical trades. At family gatherings, they boast of rewiring their own houses, building additions all by themselves, and so forth. Stan's own accomplishments as a poet and librarian are ignored when they're not being actively derided. His family does not regard mental labor as real work, man's work. When the kitchen sink springs a leak, Stan feels it as a personal challenge to his virility. His inability to repair the sink arouses in him a hot, familiar sense of humiliation. He experiences Kate's suggestion to call a plumber as a further affront.

It isn't Kate's fault that Stan is feeling emasculated, and there's not a thing she can do about it. He'll feel diminished if she calls a plumber. He'll feel diminished if she fixes the sink herself. He'll feel diminished if she just puts a bucket under the leak and resigns herself to living with it. She can't win. The leaky sink is arousing in Stan feelings that have nothing to do with her, the sink, or their relationship. He is in the throes of his familiar.

The last time this happened, Kate had an intuition about what Stan was feeling. Instead of blowing up, she said gently, "Look, sweetie, I couldn't care less that you don't know how to fix the sink. If that's what I wanted in a guy, I'd have married a handyman instead of a poet. A plumber I can always find in the yellow pages. Poets are harder to come by."

Stan's response was to hurl a pipe wrench across the room in fury.

If it were possible for one partner to heal the other's familiar, then Kate's remark should have done the trick. She was letting Stan know that she respected him for who he really was, that not being able to fix the sink didn't make him any less of a man in her eyes. You might expect hearing that to make him feel better. Instead, he felt even more upset. This bewildering response to getting what one really needs is not uncommon. You've probably reacted that way yourself on occasion and seen your partner do so. What's going on when that happens?

When their needs are denied or dismissed, children often blame themselves. To be angry with a parent or another significant adult is frightening to children. They subconsciously believe that their anger has the power to drive the parent away, resulting in their own abandonment. When you are a child, it is less frightening to believe that you are inadequate than it is to believe that your parent is inadequate. So when Stan's parents neglected to foster his intellectual gifts, Stan rationalized his disappointment by believing what his brothers' teasing had always implied—that he was some sort of a freak. As an adult, he finds himself under a sink unable to do what his brothers can do about sinks and feels that what he can do instead is of little value.

Kate chooses that moment to tell him how highly she esteems his real gifts and how little she cares about the abilities he lacks. This is good news. But to rejoice in it, Stan would have to admit how disappointed he is that no one in his family has ever said to him what Kate is saying. What gets to him is the contrast between this good thing happening in the present and a bad thing that happened constantly in the past. The contrast is poignant. It makes him sad. We call this feeling "the contrast place."

Greta was in a contrast place when Dave made a concerted effort to stop interrupting her. Instead of seizing the opportunity to have her say, she found herself falling silent. She was receiving from Dave what she'd always needed, but her first response was to feel despondent. In the moment of finally being listened to, she was overwhelmed with the sorrow that she'd felt all of the times that she wasn't listened to in the past. Similarly, on the night of the Great Chicken Soup Fight, Morrie couldn't take it that Arleah was willing, able, and eager to provide the kind of homecoming he'd always longed for as a child. The contrast only made him feel his childhood disappointment more acutely.

Have you ever found yourself inexplicably depressed right after attaining something you've always wanted? What you are experiencing is the contrast place. Beneath many of the dreams that we pursue is a yearning to console or vindicate the child we once were. We hope that attaining a desire in the present will make up for a childhood disappointment. We hope that an adult achievement will finally bring us the recognition that we longed for as kids. But nothing we attain as adults ever quite fills the old emptiness. Even if the parent whose favor you craved finally does bestow it on you in the wake of your adult achievement, their praise doesn't delight you as you always imagined it would. You needed it *then,* when you were little. Now that you're grown, it's not the same. Nothing you attain as an adult can change your childhood or assuage your early disappointments. The moment of attainment is when that reality hits you. It's why you may find yourself feeling low when you would seem to have every good reason to feel great.

Crying over Spilled Milk

Even though our partners are not responsible, the fact remains that relationships become painful when our familiars are triggered. If working on our relationship isn't the answer, what are we supposed to do instead?

Behind every familiar is a deep sense of loss. As long as that loss remains unmourned, the feelings accompanying it will have tremendous power over our behavior in the present. In order to reduce the familiar's hold on us, we need to re-experience the loss from the past so that we can release the pent-up feelings and move on. In other words, we need to grieve.

When we first made this suggestion to Stan, he became indignant. "Don't start with me about the 'inner child,'" he said. "I've never been a whiner, and I'm not going to start now. My parents did just fine, thank you very much. *You* try raising ten kids on a cabdriver's wages."

To blame parents or to label our families of origin "abusive" or "dysfunctional" has become a therapeutic cliché. People like Stan who value personal responsibility often have an aversion to attributing their present feelings and behavior to what their parents did or failed to do. As Stan went on to say, "Nobody has an ideal childhood."

He's right. Nobody has an ideal childhood. Parents don't have to be mean, crazy, or neglectful to disappoint their children. In fact, if they'd never disappointed you, you'd probably be in prison right now. It is a parent's duty to teach us that we can't have everything we want the minute that we want it. It is our parents' job to civilize us. To be disappointed as a child is the predictable result of normal, healthy, responsible parenting.

That doesn't mean that it doesn't hurt. If someone disappoints us as an adult, we have the option of getting our needs met elsewhere. We do not—if we are thinking like adults—conclude that our needs will always go unmet just because a particular individual has let us down. Children, lacking this perspective, take disappointment hard. They draw exaggerated conclusions from it. Childhood is painful for everyone. You are not putting down your parents when you acknowledge that. How you turn out as an adult has less to do with what actually happened when you were a child than with how you *felt* about what happened and how you relate to those feelings now that you are grown.

We asked Stan to describe what he had appreciated about his upbringing and what strengths he had as a result of it.

"One thing my parents did right was to get me a library card the minute I learned to read. I remember how powerful I felt the first time I checked out a stack of Little Golden Books. To me, that was like being rich. They couldn't afford to buy us a lot of toys, so we had to invent ways to play without them. I had to use my imagination more than most kids, and I guess that's why I've got such a good one. Because we were poor, I learned to appreciate things that money can't buy."

"That's what makes you such a good poet," Kate observed. "Your imagination, your ability to appreciate the little things. . . . I love those qualities in you."

"Yeah, maybe so. Ironic isn't it? My parents didn't have any use for poets, but they managed to raise one. They did a pretty good job of it."

"How did you conclude that they had no use for poets?" Arleah asked.

"Well, for one thing, whenever she caught me reading or writing, my mom would give me chores to do. That was reasonable. I was the oldest, but. . . ."

"But?"

"But there was always this implication that I was lazy, that I wasn't worth anything unless I was doing chores. I remember in eighth grade, I won a school prize for an essay I'd written. When I came home and told her about it, she was trying to cook dinner and something or other was wrong with the stove, so all she said was, 'That's nice. Can you go down and check the fuse box?' Well, what was I expecting? A parade? Only, the next year, my little brother won a wrestling tournament, and we had a little family party to celebrate. She baked a cake. So I guess I wished she'd baked a cake for me. Isn't that dumb?"

"No, it isn't dumb," Kate said. "I wish she'd baked a cake for you, too. That's a really sad story, Stan."

"You baked me a cake once. Remember? When I got that Arts Council grant."

"You were none too pleased. All you said was, 'How are the two of us ever going to eat all this?'"

"I know. I was mean about it. I don't know why. But you see, I still remember it after all these years. When I think about it now, I feel touched."

Kate's cake, like her remark when Stan was trying to repair the sink, had put Stan in a contrast place. That's why he responded churlishly at the time. Having been constantly thwarted in his desire to be recognized by his parents for his literary talents, he had learned to suppress the desire. He told himself that he didn't need or want his achievements to be celebrated. To take pleasure in Kate's cake would have meant admitting that he did want to be celebrated after all. It would have meant reopening the wound of his boyhood disappointment. Once he acknowledged the loss that made her gesture a contrast place for him, he was able to receive the affection behind it. In retrospect, at least, he was able to feel happy about it.

How to Grieve

You probably think of grieving as what people do when they experience a major loss, such as a death. No one has to tell you how to grieve then, for your sadness arises quite naturally, even uncontrollably. People around you acknowledge your loss. They send flowers, sympathy cards, and casseroles. They let you know that you are *entitled* to mourn. Your loss is official, and you have social permission to be sad.

Grieving may sound to you like an exaggerated response to the remembered disappointments of an ordinary childhood. Outwardly, nothing unusual has happened. Your loss is unofficial. People around you do not acknowledge it as your loss now that you are an adult, and it probably wasn't acknowledged when you were a child, either. No one has told you that you are entitled to feel sad. In fact, you have probably gathered quite the opposite impression. Most of us have been taught to suppress our sorrow over the losses and disappointments of everyday life. We deny our sadness so habitually that grieving no longer comes naturally to us. We don't know how to go about it.

When we don't know how to grieve directly, we do so indirectly. Stan was grieving indirectly when he threw the pipe wrench. He knew he felt awful, but he didn't know that his feeling was really sadness, and he didn't know *why* he was sad. Kate had a pretty good hunch, but since Stan himself didn't know, he was unable to receive the comfort she offered. His indirect grief put distance between them.

To grieve directly is to experience your sadness as sadness, to express it and acknowledge its source. Stan was grieving directly when he described what had happened to him in eighth grade and how he felt about it. His *indirect* grief was inconsolable, but once he grieved openly, he was able to feel the comfort that Kate extended to him. Sharing his grief brought them closer.

If you find it difficult to grieve directly, then the first step you need to take is to identify what you are doing instead. Very few children are encouraged by their parents to experience their sadness fully. What you were taught to do instead is probably what you're still doing as an adult. Here are some of the most common stratagems for avoiding the direct experience of grief:

- *Getting angry instead.* This is especially true of men since many little boys are taught that it is unmanly to cry. Our culture tends to be more accepting of open expressions of anger in boys and men. If you were raised this way, then you tend to believe that you are angry—and to make yourself angry—whenever you are unhappy. Cursing, yelling, or hitting something may produce an immediate physical release, enabling you to "get rid of" what you're feeling before you have a chance to experience and reflect on its true source.

- *Blaming someone else.* It might be your partner, your parents, an opposing political party, or an anonymous driver who has cut you off. Blame is akin to anger, but instead of releasing your emotion, you rationalize it. You start building a case in your head about how wrong someone else is. You probably learned to do this in a home where debates and arguments were substituted for open expressions of emotion.

- *Blaming yourself.* You tell yourself that your feelings are petty. You call yourself a wimp, a whiner, or a wuss. You exhort yourself to snap out of it. If this is how you typically react, then you can probably remember being reproached for your disappointment when you were a child. Perhaps you were told that you were "spoiled" or reminded that others had it worse.

- *Excusing the other person.* If you do this a lot, then you probably label it "forgiveness" and consider it a virtue in yourself. But you are not truly forgiving if you don't acknowledge that you feel hurt. When your first impulse is to make excuses for someone who has disappointed you, then you are rationalizing about the situation instead of feeling. You may have developed this stratagem as a child if expressing your disappointment seemed to hurt a parent's feelings. Rather than risk hurting someone else, you tend to deny your own experience.

- *Distraction.* The disappointment of infants and small children is very noisy. Since almost all parents attempt to distract their screaming kids on occasion, self-distraction as a remedy for grief is almost universal in adults. You put a pacifier in your mouth—a drink, a snack, or a smoke. Or you numb out in front of the TV or the computer. Maybe you meditate or work out—healthy habits that are nevertheless a dodge if you're using them to avoid your feelings.

- *Histrionics.* For some parents, giving in to a child's tantrums is the most expedient way of putting a stop to the bombastic expression of their feelings. Their children learn that throwing a fit will get them what they want and enable them to avoid the experience of disappointment. While bullies and tragedy queens may appear to be in touch with their feelings, they seldom achieve a genuine catharsis or get to the bottom of what's bothering them. Acting out becomes a substitute for feeling.

Once you've identified your strategy for dodging sadness, the next step is to stop yourself from doing it. When you catch yourself ranting, building a case in your head, making excuses for someone else, zoning out in front of the TV, or mindlessly feeding your face, stop for a moment. Let whatever happens next wash over you without trying to resist it. Just sit there and be with yourself for a few minutes.

As you learn to connect with what you are feeling in the present, its familiar quality will begin to strike you. Remembering other times when you've felt the same way will lead you back to the childhood origins of the emotion. What you recall will not necessarily be a big traumatic event. It is more likely to be something subtle, such as the empty feeling that Morrie used to have when he came home from school or the way Stan felt when torn away from his books to do chores. You will begin to see the relationship between the feeling memory of childhood and whatever triggered that feeling in the present.

The intensity of your grief may alarm you at first, and its persistence over time may dismay you. The sorrow most people carry into adulthood, even from what they think of as a "normal" childhood, is buried deep. To unearth it is wrenching. You have probably resisted feeling it for many years. The first time you finally face it, you may experience a catharsis. You may have a good cry and find that afterward a sense of peace comes over you. You think: What a relief to finally get that out of my system! But your relief is short-lived because once you acknowledge one loss, other losses start queuing up, clamoring for your attention. When you finally start to grieve your childhood, you find yourself grieving all of the years since, all of the years that you've been carrying that burden of unmourned loss. You begin to see how that burden has weighed you down, held you back, and sapped the present of joy. Those realizations become further sources of grief. You may wonder if you'll ever come to the end of it.

Grief is a process, not an event. A sorrow that you've been carrying all your life cannot be shrugged off in a single moment of catharsis. Your grief will heal, but you will not be able to identify the moment the healing happened. Like a physical wound, it scabs over and then bleeds anew each time the scab is disturbed. Then one day, you notice the scab has fallen away. When did it happen?

The wound doesn't bleed anymore, but the skin is still tender and pink. Later still, you examine the spot and find there's nothing left but a faint scar. Your wound has marked you, but it doesn't hurt you anymore.

It is important to express your grief—preferably to another person. Grief heals faster when it is shared. If talking about your sadness to other people doesn't come naturally to you, then you can start by expressing it privately at first. You might write a letter to the parent who disappointed you. (You don't have to mail it.) You might write in a journal or talk aloud to yourself.

Once you've gotten used to talking to yourself about your sadness, we hope you'll begin to confide in your partner. Believe us when we tell you that your partner won't consider this an imposition. Indirect grieving begets discord. Direct grieving creates closeness. You are letting your partner know you better and opening yourself to receiving comfort. Sharing your grief also shows your partner that you know she is not to blame for what you are feeling—which in many marriages comes as a great relief.

When it is your partner who is expressing grief, you might not know what to say or do. The main thing to remember is what *not* to do. Don't try to cheer up your partner. If he is sad, then he *needs* to be sad. Saying the wrong thing is always the result of trying to make another person's emotions go away. Let him fully experience what he is feeling. So long as you are truly willing to let your partner be sad, whatever you say or do will be just right.

When to Grieve

Have you ever mourned your wedding day? Grieved the birth of your first child? Expressed sorrow over a promotion and raise at work? If not, then you probably need to. Every change—even change for the better—involves loss. If you are growing today, then you are letting go of a little piece of who you were yesterday. It is important to remember to say good-bye.

When, after five years of planning our relocation, we finally moved into our dream house, we were thrilled. It was everything we'd hoped for and more. We were proud of what we'd accomplished together. Yet once we'd settled in, our relationship seemed to deteriorate. We sniped at each other over trivia and began to cherish small grievances instead of clearing the air right away, as we'd always done in the past. One night, after an especially idiotic quarrel, Morrie broke the uncomfortable silence with a sigh. "The only trouble with Montana is that you can't get a good bowl of matzo ball soup," he said.

Arleah sighed back. "What I really miss is the way the afternoon sun used to come in the kitchen window of our old house."

With that the dam burst, and we both unleashed a torrent of sadness about everything we'd left behind in

Chicago. It wasn't that we regretted our move. The new home was what we truly wanted. But in order to realize our dream, we had to let go of our old home. Each of us had been reluctant to admit to the other that we were sad about it. The grief that we tried to suppress had been leaking out in the form of irritability. Once we were able to confront it directly, we stopped fighting.

What is true of us is true of couples in general. Dumb fights are a symptom of unmourned loss. If you don't grieve a loss directly, then your sadness will seep out indirectly and poison your relationship. Grouchiness, pettiness, or a general sense of the blahs are all symptoms of underlying grief.

A commitment to personal growth produces constant losses because each time you move forward to embrace the new, you have to let go of something old. The more awake and present you are in your life, the more you will feel these losses. Every one of them needs to be grieved. Happy changes don't *feel* happy if the losses they entail are not grieved. You keep telling yourself that you're supposed to be happy and can't understand why you are not. The residue of sadness that poisons positive changes when it goes unacknowledged can, over time, lead you to be reluctant to make any change at all. You begin to get the impression that nothing really makes you happy and that change isn't worth the risk. Grieving what you've left behind is the secret to feeling genuinely happy about positive change.

Maybe this sounds grim to you. You may be getting the impression that if you follow our advice, your marriage will turn into an Irish wake. It won't. Grief carried over from the distant past feels very heavy and may take a long time to heal. But as you unburden yourself of past losses by grieving them, you begin to live more fully in the present. The everyday losses that you experience in the present seldom tear you up the way the old ones did, and your grief over them seldom lasts long. Losses in the present don't weigh you down if you acknowledge them as soon as they arise.

You say to your partner, "I realized today that I'm never again going to be able to fit into my old jeans. I'm feeling really bummed out about it." That's grieving. By the end of the day, you're over it. This is infinitely preferable to falling into a protracted mid-life funk or having an affair to convince yourself that you're still attractive—which often happens when the changes that come with aging are not grieved openly.

Paradoxical as it may seem, grieving the past is the path to happiness in the present. As you begin to connect with your individual grief, you will discover that your partner is not the true source of your negative feelings. Your partner is not a problem, and your relationship doesn't need working on after all.

myth

Selflessness and giving to others build the best relationships.

Clear limits and boundaries build mutual respect and lasting relationships.

reality

Chapter 4

Most of the stories we have to tell in this book are success stories. Most of our clients not only weather the crises that lead them to seek our help, but they come through with stronger, happier marriages. In this chapter, we're going to tell you about two marriages that ended in bitter divorce. We begin with these cautionary tales to impress on you the destructiveness of the self-sacrifice myth. Of all relationship myths, this one is the most deeply ingrained in our culture. It is also probably the single greatest obstacle to marital happiness.

Bernard and Stacy met in college, where Bernard was a pre-med student. Stacy can barely recall what her original major had been because once she fell in love, she began to major in Bernard. When they married, she dropped out of school and went to work full-time as an administrative assistant. She supported the two of them while Bernard completed his medical training, paid off his student loans, and established his practice. Once they were on their feet financially, Stacy was relieved to quit the job she'd always hated and start having babies. For the next fifteen years, she devoted herself to raising their two children and managing the household. She took pride in supporting Bernard's professional life by making domestic life easy for him. He came home to gracious and impeccable surroundings, gourmet meals, and high-achieving progeny. She managed all of their social obligations, throwing elegant dinner parties, handling Bernard's Christmas shopping, and

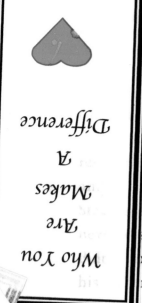

Who You Are Makes A Difference

ing to send birthday cards signed with his name is friends and relations.

did she neglect the conjugal side of their ip. She had worked hard to preserve her figure eep the romance in her marriage. Nevertheless, spected that Bernard was unfaithful. She had scovered irrefutable evidence of this, and she looking for it. Occasional evasiveness about reabouts was the main clue. Rather than her suspicions, she redoubled her efforts to be a wonderful wife and lover. She trusted that even if he strayed from time to time, Bernard would never leave her or jeopardize their marriage with a serious entanglement. She believed that to act jealous and accusing was the surest way to alienate a man. Boys will be boys, she thought with a shrug, when she thought about it at all.

As it turned out, Stacy miscalculated. One night, Bernard came home and announced that he had met someone else. The affair had been going on for more than a year, and he was deeply in love. He asked for a divorce.

If this old familiar story is boring you silly, wake up. We're going to spring a pop quiz on you. Based solely on the information that we've provided so far, let's see if you can guess the identity of Bernard's "someone else":

a.   She is a manicurist and aspiring lingerie model called Bambi.

b.   She is the perky, efficient young receptionist who charms his patients and rubs his shoulders when he returns to the office after a long day in the operating room.

c.   She is a sleek, stylish socialite who presides over the Women's Auxiliary at the hospital and gave him a very flattering introduction when he spoke at their monthly luncheon.

d.   She is a rather unkempt photojournalist, two years his senior, who put up a spirited fight when Bernard thoughtlessly climbed into a cab she'd just hailed.

Possibilities a, b, and c had all played out obsessively in Stacy's tortured fantasies. To have stolen Bernard, her rival must either be younger and prettier or even better than Stacy at what Stacy already did—catering to Bernard and making him look good. Never in her wildest nightmares could she have entertained the possibility that Bernard would leave her for a hard-driving journalist whose idea of culinary achievement was ordering a pizza and whose idea of a fashion statement was a baseball cap and sneakers. But that's what happened. Bernard fell for Barb not because she was younger, prettier, or more accommodating than his wife. She was none of that. He fell for her simply because she was so much more *interesting*.

Stacy felt bitter at what she perceived to be the injustice of this. "Sure she's interesting. I'd be interesting too if I hadn't dropped out of college to support you. I'd be interesting too if I left my kids with my mother while I went off to photograph water buffalo. I'd be plenty interesting if I were running all over the city at night instead of reheating your dinner and running your bath."

"Yes, I daresay you would be," Bernard said thoughtfully. "I wonder why that never occurred to either of us until now."

Maybe you see Stacy as a victim. If so, she is not Bernard's victim. She is a victim of the myth that selfless devotion keeps marriage alive. In fact, nothing kills a marriage faster. The brutal truth of the matter is that most of the services Stacy provided Bernard were easily replaceable. You can hire housekeepers, caterers, errand runners, and social secretaries. Only a true partner is irreplaceable. After twenty-five years of marriage, Bernard was bound to Stacy mainly by a sentimental attachment to the past and a "gratitude" that was little more than the guilty belief that he *ought* to be grateful.

As we see it, Stacy had deserted Bernard long before he announced that he was officially deserting her. In living through Bernard instead of cultivating a life of her own, she had failed to become a full person and thereby deprived him of a full partner. In catering to his every need, she had not only failed in her own growth, but also failed to challenge Bernard to grow. She had treated him like a little boy who was incapable of taking care of himself. At the age of forty-eight, Bernard didn't even know how to operate a washing machine or a coffeemaker. His domestic dependence on her and her economic dependence on him had long rendered divorce unthinkable for both of them. Yet Bernard's loneliness was so acute that when the possibility of real intimacy with another partner presented itself, he mustered up the courage to outgrow his dependency.

Stacy did not. When divorce was threatened, she redoubled her efforts to prove herself indispensable. Guilt, gratitude, and dependency were the only hold that she had on Bernard, and the desperation of these measures became more apparent once he expressed his desire to escape. Bitterly she reproached him with reminders of all she had given up for him. Yet when he confronted her with the question, "What, exactly, did you give up?" she didn't have an answer. She couldn't actually remember having ever desired anything but the role of homemaker. Marrying Bernard at a young age had enabled her to evade questions that she didn't yet know how to answer about her own identity and purpose in the world. She still didn't know the answer to those questions, but rather than grapple with them now, she focused on guilt-tripping Bernard. Her strategy backfired. After a year of enduring her reproaches, Bernard felt he'd done his penance and could live with his guilt. He gave her everything she asked for in the divorce settlement and went to live happily, if penuriously, with the woman that he'd come to consider his dearest friend.

———————————————

The story of Sebastian and Colleen is as bizarre in its specifics as the story of Bernard and Stacy is trite, but the underlying dynamics are essentially the same. In this case, it was the husband who assumed the role of sacrificial victim.

Sebastian and Colleen had always held personal growth and honest communication as shared values. Colleen was willful and independent, and Sebastian liked her that way. To see her flourishing in her own right had always gratified him. A recovering alcoholic, he had undergone a lot of personal therapy and was more forthcoming about his feelings than many husbands. The depth and candor of their exchanges was one of the true strengths of their marriage. Both expected their union to last precisely because they didn't take it for granted.

The trouble began when Colleen expressed dissatisfaction with their sex life. Sebastian was disconcerted. He had thought that it was just fine. Nevertheless, he was willing to be challenged to expand his range. When she proposed that they act out some of her fantasies, he enthusiastically agreed. Having been a theater major in college, he found in Colleen's demands an exciting new outlet for talents that had long lain dormant. Together, they scrounged thrift shops for costumes and props. For their fifteenth wedding anniversary, he outdid himself in staging Colleen's gang rape fantasy. He erected a chain link fence in the bedroom and enacted the roles of five different gang members.

Alas, being gang raped by her own husband was not enough to appease Colleen's growing appetite for sexual variety and risk. At her instigation, they plotted the seduction of other couples. It was at this point that Sebastian began to feel uncomfortable. He spent the first of these nights offering Valium and Kleenex to the distraught wife of the other couple while Colleen sported with the husband. Afraid that Colleen would be disappointed in him, he did not disclose to her that he had been feeling jealous of the other man and awkward with the woman. He agreed to another such adventure and believed he was making progress when he was able to enjoy the wife. He enjoyed her so much, in fact, that he wanted to go on seeing her. Colleen vetoed this proposal because she hadn't really hit it off with the husband. Sebastian readily capitulated, secretly relieved by the implication that the only sexual adventures permitted in the marriage were those undertaken as a couple. He figured that was the next best thing to monogamy.

They began to haunt sleazy bars, where Sebastian would strike up an acquaintance with whatever dangerous character Colleen had her eye on and invite him back to their home. He was too busy pimping for his wife to choose partners of his own, and in any case, the women who frequented such establishments were not really his type. Back at the house, he was careful to remain within earshot, lest Colleen find herself out of her depth with the thug of her choice and require rescue. As her yearning for sexual risk increased, Sebastian began to fear that she would strike out on her own and find herself in real danger. He feigned enthusiasm for their outings in the hope that she would not be tempted to leave him behind.

Sebastian rarely contemplated his own dissatisfaction with the kinky turn their lives had taken. He didn't complain—even in the privacy of his own mind—about Colleen's refusal to have anything resembling normal sex with him, his jealousy of her other partners, or his fear that Colleen was becoming seriously unbalanced. Whenever he felt anxious, he simply redoubled his efforts to provide her with what she wanted. While she might be rejecting him as a lover, he believed that as pimp he was making himself indispensable to her. However, the more he accommodated her, the more desperately unhappy she seemed.

Eventually, Colleen did find a new lover on her own initiative, and Sebastian could no longer deny that he was terrified of losing her. He insisted on meeting the other man and tried to become friends with him. Colleen's lover traipsed around the house in Sebastian's own bathrobe as Sebastian cooked breakfast for the pair. Far from being grateful for this act of self-abasement, Colleen treated him with contempt. The next time her lover visited, she insisted on spending the weekend alone with him. Rather than oblige them to go off to a hotel, Sebastian checked into one himself. That was the weekend he began to drink again after eighteen years of sobriety.

Three years later, this couple divorced. Sebastian has gained fifty pounds, lost his job, and reached a disabling stage of alcoholism. He flies the extremity of his suffering like a banner of reproach against his former wife. He tells anyone who'll listen how cruelly she used and abandoned him after he'd sacrificed everything for her. Meanwhile, Colleen surprised everyone by settling down with a rather staid law professor. Ironically, it is the limits imposed by her new husband that have enabled her to achieve a modicum of sexual satisfaction: "Sebastian and I were so fused that after a while I couldn't even see him as a separate person. He wasn't a man to me any more. He was just like . . . like some extra limb growing off me, hobbling me, getting in my way. In retrospect, I think all I was ever looking for in those brutes I used to pick up was a man I couldn't control."

Why Doormats Get Dumped

These are painful stories to relate. To Stacy and Sebastian, it appears that their former spouses exploited them for years and then heartlessly discarded them when they were all but used up. Our cultural mythology is such that Stacy and Sebastian can find plenty of sympathizers who will agree that they were betrayed. Perhaps the cruelest fact of all is that Bernard and Colleen, the "heavies" in these marriages, went on to find happiness in new unions while their partners remained bitter and unwilling to risk being hurt again. You may be tempted to conclude that life is unfair.

Actually, it's a lot more fair than it appears on the surface. Had Sebastian and Stacy been motivated by genuine altruism, they would not now be loathing their former spouses for finding happiness with others. Behind their selflessness was an implicit pact: "I'll take care of you and allow myself to be used if, in exchange, you promise never to abandon me." That was the unspoken agreement that got violated and why they feel entitled to be bitter now. When you forge such a pact, you don't have a marriage. You have a hostage crisis. The union is based on fear, not love. It is based on reciprocal weaknesses, not character and values.

To take a hostage and call that love is a lie that breeds other lies. Despite the open communication that had characterized the early years of their marriage, Sebastian began lying to Colleen—and to himself—as soon as she proposed partner-swapping. That proposal raised for him the prospect of being abandoned, and he began to lie out of desperation. He denied his jealousy, his feelings of rejection, his discomfort with their new lifestyle, and his worries about her emotional instability. His conduct during this period was deeply dishonest and therefore untrustworthy. The rage that he concealed even from himself eventually found expression in his return to the bottle. To destroy oneself is the ultimate revenge when the unspoken pact gets violated. It is the ultimate abandonment of one's partner.

While Colleen's sexual acting-out appears to have been the precipitating factor, the fault line that finally ruptured their marriage had been present from the beginning. A man who would volunteer for the humiliation Sebastian endured obviously has a greater than average fear of abandonment. If push came to shove, he had *always* been willing to abandon himself in order to hang onto his wife. As Colleen put it, they were "fused"—with the predictable result that sex stopped being exciting. She couldn't experience her husband as a member of the opposite sex because he never opposed her. Instead of a true partnership, their marriage had become a symbiotic blob.

Bernard and Stacy were likewise fused. Although Stacy was waiting up every night with his dinner, for Bernard it was as if no one was home. He felt lonely with her. Stacy was so focused on his needs that all he could see when he looked at her were his own needs being reflected back to him. He did indeed become increasingly self-centered and demanding because his demands were the only basis on which his wife seemed willing to relate to him. It is hardly any wonder that he became attracted to a woman who protested hotly when he tried to take her cab. Barb's self-assertion gave her a quality of otherness that never ceased to fascinate him. Paradoxically, it was her separateness that kept him from feeling lonely with her. There was always someone home.

How Marriages Turn into Symbiotic Blobs

Symbiosis with our mothers when we are infants is a condition on which our very lives depend. If mother does not intuit and meet the needs that we are not able to articulate in words, then we will die. We are as dependent on her affection as we are on her physical ministrations because infants who are not cuddled and paid attention to fail to thrive and sometimes literally die. Sebastian's mother, who suffered from severe postpartum depression after his birth, rejected him in infancy. Like all children, he believed that he was to blame for his mother's feelings. As an adult, he persists in a deep-seated, unexamined conviction that if he is emotionally abandoned, then he deserves to die. He has since gone on to demonstrate it with a slow, self-inflicted death from alcoholism.

Few mothers are as inadequate as Sebastian's. Most of us have gotten our symbiotic needs met in infancy to some extent. If they are fully met, we outgrow them naturally and move of our own accord toward greater independence. This natural process goes awry when a mother attempts either to hasten or to resist it. Many of us have troubled familiars around symbiosis. Some of us haven't gotten quite enough and carry an unfulfilled longing into adulthood. Others of us picked up on our mother's anxiety or resistance when we began to assert independence and have been anxious about asserting independence ever since.

The early stages of falling in love are a blissful return to symbiosis. We become the center of our beloved's attention and they, the center of ours. We seem to read each other's minds, never tire of each other's company, and find even each other's flaws and idiosyncrasies utterly adorable. Eventually, this wears off. That is the first major loss that we go through with our partners. It is sad, and it needs to be grieved. Yet it is essential that we experience this loss. The high-maintenance honeymoon phase lays the foundation of closeness that makes for a satisfying low-maintenance relationship later on. The partnership that will see us through the rigors and responsibilities of adult life can't really begin until we get past the symbiotic stage. A great many marital problems can be traced to the reluctance to part with a symbiosis that has passed its expiration date. The milk gradually curdles and sours, but we refuse to throw it out.

We've described two symbiotic marriages in which the care-taking role consistently fell to one partner. In other marriages, the care-taking role keeps shifting. He takes care of her during her crisis; a few months later he has a crisis, and she takes care of him. Such marriages tend to face many crises because staging an inner or outer emergency is the only way to get out of the care-taking role when it begins to grow tiresome. Couples like this believe that their relationship is reciprocal, exhibits a healthy give-and-take pattern because each gets to have a turn being the baby. The symptom that the relationship is actually a symbiotic blob is that the couple doesn't experience closeness except when in crisis. Complication and drama become a substitute for intimacy.

Is your marriage a symbiotic blob? Here are some of the telltale signs:

- Your partner asks, "What do you feel like doing tonight?" You reply, "I don't know. What do you feel like doing?" Or vice versa. Each of you is so concerned with pleasing the other that you can't seem to come up with any desires of your own. Until you hear what your partner wants, you truly don't know what you want.

- You can't make even minor decisions without consulting your partner—or your partner can't make a decision without consulting you. Either one person makes all the decisions or else each defers to the other to such an extent that no decisions get made at all.

- You do all of your socializing as a couple. If you meet someone you like and your partner doesn't like her, then you don't pursue the friendship.
- One of you consistently tries to control the other. The controlling partner ridicules the other's personal tastes and interests, and the submissive partner gives up liking whatever the controlling partner disdains. The controlling partner constantly offers unsolicited advice about matters that any grown-up can figure out for himself.
- One or both of you is given to irrational bouts of jealousy. You feel threatened if your partner develops a crush on a movie star, or your partner feels threatened if you become friends with a member of the opposite sex. The possibility that your partner could feel even a casual attraction to someone else strikes you as utterly catastrophic.
- If your partner is angry or disappointed with you, you can't feel better until your partner feels better. If your partner seems unhappy in general, you assume it's your fault.
- You are deeply dissatisfied with some important aspect of your life—what you do for a living, where you live, dreams and aspirations you've allowed to fall by the wayside, and so forth—and blame this circumstance on your marriage. You believe your partner's happiness depends on the sacrifice of what you yourself desire.

- You feel that the independent actions of your partner reflect on you. If your partner wears a striped shirt with plaid pants or tells a joke that falls flat, then you feel personally embarrassed. If your partner offends someone you know, then you feel responsible for setting things right.

- Even now that you are grown, you feel afraid of disappointing one or both of your parents. You allow yourself to be controlled by the displeasure of family members. Adults who have not declared independence from their families of origin tend to form symbiotic relationships with their spouses.

What all of these symbiosis symptoms have in common is an underlying belief that one partner's self-assertion will hurt the other and damage the relationship. If asked why you allow any of these undesirable conditions to continue, you respond by describing your partner rather than yourself. You offer your partner as the explanation for what you are thinking, feeling, or doing. If pressed further, you eventually come round to the argument that to assert yourself would be selfish.

The Selfishness Taboo

There is no quicker way to shame someone than to call her selfish. The word "selfish" has a downright magical power to stop most people in their tracks. The taboo against acting in one's own best interest runs so deep in our culture that merely to apply the word "selfish" to another's actions is to make an open-and-shut case that she is in the wrong.

Throughout most of human history, the taboo against selfishness has been essential for survival. The individual was dependent on the clan or tribe. To think, feel, or act contrary to the interests of the tribe was to risk banishment, and this was, in a very real sense, to risk death. In celebrating altruism, humanity was simply making a virtue of necessity.

For contemporary Americans, survival no longer depends on subordinating one's needs to a particular tribe. We still need other people, to be sure, but we are free to choose our affiliations. If you find yourself at odds with one group, you can seek out another more to your liking. You don't have to fit into any pre-existing group at all. You can put yourself at the center of a network of your own creation. Your Rolodex is the membership roster of your own self-defined "tribe."

The hold of the old tribal mythology is such that for many of us this thought is a little bit sad, if not downright frightening. Many of us are nostalgic for the idealized memory of the extended family, the small town, the ethnic ghetto, and the company that keeps you on the payroll during a recession and presents you with a gold watch upon retirement. In our longing for roots and the imagined intimacy that comes with them, we tend to forget what made us want to pull up our roots in the first place. We forget what these old affiliations used to cost the individual—the suppression of differences, the pressure to conform, and to think small and be small. Most of us don't really want to live under the same roof with our aunts, uncles, and grandparents, nor do we want our every move to be the subject of small-town or ghetto gossip.

What we truly long for is intimacy. You won't find it in your tribal past. It never really existed there. The intimacy that you long for is something new in human history, a possibility that we who enjoy an unprecedented degree of affluence and social mobility are only just now beginning to pursue. Real intimacy arises in the relationships we form by choice rather than necessity. It is the ability to sustain these relationships without the loss of self. It is being known and accepted for who you truly are.

Real intimacy is hardy. It can survive you saying what's on your mind and in your heart. It can weather the constant changes and challenges that you provoke in your quest for personal growth. Tribalism was never that hardy. The essential fragility of a static, self-contained community had to be reinforced with taboos. It is those taboos that are still haunting you when to be called "selfish" paralyzes you with shame.

Learning to tell the difference between remorse and shame is essential to the new intimacy. When we act contrary to our values, we feel remorse—and so we should. Remorse is a reliable indicator that a core value is being violated. It is a feeling, but it is also rational. You can explain why you have it. If you identify what you believe you are doing wrong and make the necessary correction, then remorse goes away. Shame has a different quality. You can't explain it in terms of your values, nor does acting in accordance with your values necessarily make it go away. Unexamined shame even has the power to make you act *against* your values.

Shame is rooted in the fear of being abandoned. We risk being abandoned every time we assert ourselves. To declare, "I am a self" is at the same time to say, "I am not you. I am separate from you." Whether we are conscious of it or not, the implication is always, "As a separate person, you might leave me. As a separate person, I might leave you."

We first experience shame as toddlers, when we begin to experiment with the word "No." To say "No" is to declare a separate self. (As every toddler knows, Descartes's postulate should have been, "I throw tantrums, therefore I am.") Parents respond to this developmental stage with some ambivalence. Two-year-olds are not easy to live with. So along with our discovery of "No," we have our first experience of parental displeasure. Mother seems less enchanted with us than she used to be when we were infants. There are moments when we get the distinct impression that she'd rather be elsewhere. If mother really goes elsewhere, we will not survive. We feel ourselves to be in danger of being abandoned, and we feel in some obscure way that it is our own fault, that it is our self-assertion that is alienating her.

No parent can avoid feeling briefly antagonized by a toddler. Antagonizing parents is, for the child, a necessary developmental task. When all goes well, the parent's irritation is fleeting. The affection between parent and child is quickly and easily restored. The child learns from this that self-assertion will not result in abandonment and that conflict does not lead to the permanent loss of affection. Trouble arises only if the child can't find any way back into a parent's good graces after a conflict. For a toddler, an hour "in the doghouse" is an eternity. A child who experiences protracted periods of parental withdrawal begins to conclude that self-assertion *does* lead to abandonment and that he himself is to blame for it.

Such children carry their conclusion into adult life as an unexamined conviction that asserting themselves will damage or destroy relationships. On an emotional level, they are experiencing fear of abandonment. This feeling is often rationalized, developed into something that appears to be a principle. We say, "It is wrong to be selfish." The emotional subtext of that statement is, "I will be abandoned if I assert myself, and I will have it coming to me."

The statement "It is wrong to be selfish" does not hold up well to rational examination. Implicit in it is the idea that if you act in your own interest, you are acting contrary to everyone else's. This is, in fact, true of two-year-olds. It is not true of adults. Healthy, sane adults are capable not only of saying "No," but also of taking "No" for an answer. We do not, as a rule, coerce others into giving us our way, nor do we immediately abandon those who refuse. Having a self does not turn the average adult into Attila the Hun.

The belief that to assert yourself is to hurt others is rooted in shame, which is in turn rooted in the fear of being abandoned. The reality is that you probably won't be abandoned for asserting yourself. Furthermore, if you *are* abandoned, you will survive it. As a child, you could not have survived the loss of your parents' good will. As an adult, you can lose the good will of any other adult and live to tell the tale. As an adult, the only abandonment that can kill you is *self*-abandonment.

Asserting Your Boundaries

We've been talking tough in this chapter because to stand up against the prevailing cultural mythology of self-sacrifice requires a strong countervailing value. We want to make it very clear that it is the *failure* to assert oneself that puts marriages in jeopardy and that if you abandon yourself, you are abandoning your partner as well. If what you have been calling a marriage is really a symbiotic blob, then it is doomed in the long run. To save it will require courageous assertion of your own boundaries and limits.

How do you go about asserting a limit? It's simple (though by no means easy). You just say "No." What people usually mean when they ask, "*How* do I say 'No?'" is "How do I say 'No' without upsetting my partner?" Our clients often want us to offer them a painless formula. There is none. Changing a symbiotic status quo is likely to upset your partner at some point. She is likely to resist, and you are likely to feel bad when she does. There is no way to change a relationship for the better without enduring pain and risk.

Shame is too deeply rooted in our psyches and our culture to disappear overnight. In risking self-assertion, you are risking shame. You can't navigate around it. Instead, you've got to go *through* it—experiencing the shame and discovering that you can survive it.

When we take an emotional risk, the backlash of shame follows a predictable pattern. Here's what you're in for:

1. Your first reaction is likely to be implosion. Ever seen a film of a building being demolished by explosives? It collapses in on itself. That's how you feel. The courage that led you to assert yourself in the first place seems to have blown itself to dust, and you're left feeling like a heap of rubble. Even in the absence of a negative response from the other person, this inward state feels like a bad result.

2. Since you've gotten this bad inner result, it must be that you've done something wrong. You reproach and blame yourself. You begin to doubt whatever it is that you were asserting. You feel tempted to take it back, or at least water it down.

3. You get a vague sense of impending doom and feel as if something terrible has happened or is about to happen. This sense of doom may not be consciously connected with the risk you have just taken. The catastrophe that you imagine might not have anything to do with your partner's real or imagined response. You might instead worry that you forgot to unplug the iron, fear that an oncoming car is going to hit you, or that one of your children is in danger. All you know is that something's not right with your world.

4. The final stage is retreat. Until you know the outcome of the risk that you have taken, you are unable to take any further risks. During this period, you become more cautious than usual.

How the other person actually responds has no bearing on this sequence of emotions. It goes on in your own head irrespective of your partner's response. It is a familiar—a feeling from the past that comes over you regardless of how things are going in the present.

We have even worse news. No matter how your partner responds, you're likely to feel bad when the actual outcome becomes clear. If he responds negatively, then you feel confirmed in the belief that you never should have taken the risk in the first place. If he responds positively (a more likely outcome than you probably imagine), then you may be thrown into a "contrast place." All of your life you've been thinking that you couldn't get away with the risk you've just taken, and now you discover that you can. While thrilling, this discovery also opens up regret over all of the times that you've avoided risk in the past or taken a risk and suffered for it.

When we take an emotional risk, we are parting company with our familiar. The familiar self feels abandoned by this new self that we are becoming, and the new self feels—well, *unfamiliar.* We feel a bit unsteady, a bit out of control. We don't even know what *we* are going to do next, much less what our partner is going to do.

In short, we can pretty much guarantee that you're going to feel awful as soon as you begin to assert yourself in unaccustomed ways. With such a grim prognosis, you may be wondering why on earth anyone would want to do it. Happily, the long-term results are a great deal more favorable than the short-term discomfort that we are predicting. In letting your partner know where your boundaries are, you are extending an invitation to full partnership and deeper intimacy. Your partner isn't an idiot. She can perceive this, even if your self-assertion is initially disconcerting. Recall how Dave responded to Greta's refusal to come to bed on demand. Stating her boundaries enabled him to experience his own. He felt more secure with her and more attracted to her. Recall how crazy Colleen got when Sebastian refused to state his own limits and how relieved she was to find a new partner who demanded that she behave more responsibly.

If worse comes to worst, your partner will indeed reject you. This is far less likely than you imagine, but it can happen. If it does—well, the good news is that we're not attending your funeral. Adults do not die when they are rejected or abandoned. When your worst fear comes to pass, it stops being your worst fear. Ultimately, you have nothing to lose but your own timidity.

Having said all this, we do have one piece of practical advice to impart. We recommend that you start small. Don't set yourself up for failure by demanding drastic, sudden changes. Stacy would have pretty much guaranteed a negative outcome if she'd suddenly announced to Bernard that he'd better hire a housekeeper because she was joining the Peace Corps and moving to Ecuador. But he probably could have taken it in stride if she'd said, "I'm going to be taking a class at the community college two nights a week. Let me show you how to operate the microwave."

We'd also like to point out that you don't necessarily have to begin with your partner. If you have been avoiding self-assertion in your marriage, then you probably avoid it in other relationships as well. You can begin taking emotional risks in relationships that you have less fear of losing. If, as an adult, you still have difficulty standing up to one of your parents, that's an excellent place to start.

Finding Your Boundaries

One of the toughest challenges in asserting boundaries is figuring where they are—or where they're supposed to be—in the first place. The whole trouble with a symbiotic relationship is that you don't know. You've lost all track of where your partner leaves off and you begin. You're not really clear on where to draw the line between reasonable give-and-take and self-abdication.

When we violate our core values, we violate our boundaries as well. By concentrating on living our values, we're able to see pretty clearly where our limits are. For example, if you value wholehearted commitment to your own mission in life, then it will impose a natural limit on the extent to which you are willing to become your spouse's nanny, therapist, or sex slave. You've got to get up in the morning. If you value accountability, then there's a limit to how far you'll go to rescue a self-destructive partner. Valuing quality communication implies that you will not lie about your feelings to please your partner. Believing that the marriage relationship takes precedence over all others is all the ground you need for refusing to condone your partner's infidelity.

We're not going to draw you a map, and you don't need to draw a map, either. Personal boundaries are not like the borders between countries. They are permeable, and they fluctuate to some extent. For years, complying with Morrie's Ten Point Checklist of Kitchen Cleanliness was perfectly okay with Arleah. One night, it suddenly stopped being okay. The proposition that it is no longer okay doesn't have to be defended in a court of law. There is no judge to rule that, having complied with the Ten Point Checklist in the past, Arleah established a legal precedent and is now required to go on complying for the rest of her life. Goofy as it sounds, many couples attempt to argue that. Their willingness to cater to each other as newlyweds becomes an implicit contract, the breaking of which is treated as a betrayal.

You are entitled to change your mind about what you will and won't do for your partner. In fact, we will go so far as to say that if you never change your mind, then you are failing to grow and sentencing your marriage to death.

Chapter 5

Miranda says that she loves Derek unconditionally. This is lucky for Derek because he has a lot of unattractive traits. He belches and farts in polite company. He dribbles food down his shirt when he eats. When he wakes up in a bad mood, he insists that Miranda get up, too. He doesn't engage in conversation with her. He has never picked up a tab. His idea of an affectionate gesture is pulling Miranda's hair. Since she became involved with Derek, Miranda rarely leaves the house. He demands so much of her that she's had to put her career on hold. Nevertheless, Miranda is enthralled with him. She says that she never knew what love was until Derek came into her life. He is the center of her existence, and she is the center of his. She insists that theirs is a healthy relationship. It may surprise you to hear that we wholeheartedly agree.

Derek is a newborn baby. Miranda is his mother.

Unconditional acceptance is an appropriate response to someone who suffers from the temporary embarrassment of being a baby. Nobody would survive infancy if being loved depended on his merits. But somehow we've gotten it into our heads that a mother's love for her newborn is the ideal model for all other loves. Love means never having to say you're sorry. Love means never having to tuck in your shirt. Love means being accepted exactly the way you are.

This philosophy is fine if you want your marriage to become an emotional welfare state. That's what you get when love becomes an entitlement, when your partner doesn't have to do or be anything remotely loveable to be awarded your love. Put your partner on the emotional welfare roll—or expect your partner to put you there—and you'll find yourself living in a relationship slum.

We realize that this idea may be new to you. "Unconditional love" is a sacred cow in our culture, and many marriage counselors and authors of self-help books will tell you that believing you can change your partner is a fatal error. They will tell you that if you think a trait that bothers you when you're courting is going to get better after the wedding, then you're just plain crazy. What you see before the wedding is what you're going to get forever after.

This notion has the ring of common sense, and the observation of other couples tends to confirm it. Whatever was bad during the engagement tends only to get worse after the honeymoon. Nevertheless, the idea that your partner will never change to please you is inherently illogical. Think about it. When you met your partner, she was single. Now she is married. Changes don't come much bigger than that, and it happened because you wanted it to.

If you're like most couples, your attraction to each other is a mixture of healthy and unhealthy feeling patterns rooted in the past (i.e., your familiars). Part of you wishes to remain in denial about your negative familiars because examining them is so painful. That part of you approaches marriage as an unwritten emotional contract that reads, "I promise not to challenge you if you promise not to challenge me." The damaged side of you is all for going on emotional welfare and getting loved unconditionally so that you never have to reopen your wounds of grief. That's the part that therapists are looking at when they say that you can't change your partner. Their assumption is that if you've made this unconscious pact and been drawn to your partner's familiars out of your own reciprocal familiars, then you are stuck now with the consequences.

What this ignores is the part of you that is *healthy*. Your past has endowed you with gifts as well as wounds. *Your* gifts are attracted to *your partner's* gifts. The part of you that is healthy was drawn to your partner's finest qualities and hoped that those qualities would continue to develop after you got married. You were also attracted because your partner seemed to bring out the best in you and would spur you on to keep being that best. The part of you that got married for this reason will be deeply disappointed if your partner doesn't grow or doesn't challenge you to grow.

While all marriages contain some element of an unhealthy contract, an unspoken agreement not to challenge each other, our healthiest selves will feel ripped off if that contract comes to dominate. Not to challenge your partner to change is letting him down big time. It means that you don't really care. It means that you are essentially giving up on him. Failure to challenge your partner is, like selflessness, a form of emotional abandonment.

What You Have to Gain from Challenging Your Partner

In our last chapter, we described two marriages that ended badly. Let's pretend that there's a parallel universe where these couples seized the crucial opportunities to challenge each other that they had, in reality, allowed to pass.

One Valentine's Day, when Bernard came home late, as usual, Stacy met him at the door in her prettiest dress. The kids had been put to bed, and the dining room table was laid with their best linens, silver, and china. The room was lit only by candles, and sultry jazz was playing on the stereo. "Uh-oh," Bernard thought. This was his cue that he was supposed to be feeling romantic. He was tired and wanted only to flop on the couch and watch a basketball game. Hiding his dismay behind a wan smile, he sat down at the table. Mindlessly, he helped himself to the napkin that was wadded up in the wineglass in some peculiar way. Stacy's face fell. He had failed to appreciate that the wad was supposed to be a linen rosebud. Every item on the elaborate menu was either pink or heart-shaped. There were heart-shaped biscuits garnished with heart-shaped pats of butter. Dessert—a molded strawberry mousse—was *both* pink and heart-shaped. After his initial gaffe with the napkin rose, Bernard was careful to marvel over the heart-shaped ice cubes in his water glass. Secretly he was thinking, "Woman, have you lost your mind?"

That's what actually happened. Now let's replay the scene as it might have happened if Bernard had been willing to challenge Stacy with a more honest response.

He sits down graciously enough at the table. He helps himself to the napkin, spreads the butter on his biscuit, and sucks on an ice cube without producing the expected compliments on Stacy's artistic achievement. She grows silent and pouts. He asks, "What's wrong?" She says, "You don't appreciate me. You never appreciate me," and goes on to point out all of the Valentine's Day flourishes that he has overlooked.

Bernard leans across the table and takes her hand. "My dear, I see that you've gone to a great deal of trouble, and I'm sorry that my reaction has disappointed you. But can I tell you what I'm really thinking right now?"

Stacy nods, apprehensively.

"I'm just wondering, you see, whether carving butter and ice cubes into little hearts is really a suitable occupation for a grown woman. You say you've done all this for me, but I don't really care what shape the butter is. I never understand where you're coming from when you do things like this."

After a moment of stark shock, Stacy bursts into angry tears. She accuses him of belittling her and trivializing her achievements. She cites many examples. She concludes her tirade with, "You think what I do is so much less important than what you do."

"Stacy," Bernard says calmly, "performing a triple bypass operation *is* more important than folding napkins into the shape of flowers."

Maybe you're wondering if *we've* lost our minds. This scenario hardly seems like an improvement over the one that actually happened. Stacy is hurt, and the two of them have embarked on a major quarrel that might easily have been prevented if Bernard had offered the compliment that Stacy obviously craved from him. Worse, he responds to her feelings of inferiority by telling her that her accomplishments are indeed inferior to his own.

Well, they are. For Bernard to pretend otherwise would be deeply condescending, if not downright contemptuous. What's bothering Stacy—the inequality in their relationship—is very real. Bernard is dedicated to a purpose that spurs him to strive, grow, and make a significant contribution to the world outside their marriage. Stacy is dedicated to nothing except Bernard. That she caters to him with more energy and flair than is strictly necessary does not alter the dismal fact that catering to him is her only mission in life. Bernard's response may seem harsh, but it is also respectful. He is acknowledging that Stacy isn't crazy to feel diminished: She has put herself in a diminished position. To acknowledge this frankly implies that he believes she is capable of doing otherwise. There is an implicit compliment in what he is saying. He is telling her that she is made for better things.

Stacy cries herself to sleep that night. Over the next few weeks, she is cold and withdrawn. She attempts to punish Bernard by offering him microwaved frozen dinners instead of the gourmet meals to which he has grown accustomed. That he doesn't seem to mind only increases her frustration. Too angry to communicate with her husband, she begins pouring her feelings into a journal. She writes about how much she hates her life and how empty she feels when her extravagant efforts to please Bernard fail to make any impression on him. When she tries to blame him for this in writing, her words ring false to her. She is struck by the truth of what he has been saying to her lately—that he never asked her to subordinate herself to him as she has done. She begins to wonder why she has chosen to do it. She begins to face the fact that she has never been able to figure out what to do instead.

On Valentine's Day a year later, Bernard once again comes home to an extravagant display on the dining room table. But this time Stacy is in jeans, and a photographer is bustling around the room with a light meter. As Bernard has been surprised to learn, sculpting butter is indeed a suitable occupation for a grown-up. Stacy has become a freelance food stylist. Magazines and ad agencies pay her rather handsomely to treat mashed potatoes and gravy as Michelangelo treated marble. She greets him absently and tells him that there are fresh cold cuts in the fridge. He makes himself a sandwich and retires to the den to watch basketball.

Discovering a purpose beyond their marriage has turned Stacy into a new woman. If she's home when he comes home in the evening—often she isn't—then she's bursting with funny anecdotes or creative ideas related to her latest assignment. Her professional world couldn't be more different from his own, and he has come to find it interesting. Their parties are attended by a whole new crowd of artsy types that Stacy has met on the job. She has put Bernard on notice that from now on he'll have to manage his own social correspondence and Christmas shopping; she doesn't have time. When he's not eating leftovers from her photo shoots, he makes do with sandwiches and frozen dinners. When he complains of this, she offers to teach him how to cook. He takes her up on it. Cooking, he discovers, is not as easy as she always made it look. He begins to think that she's some kind of a genius after all.

One day, he gets into a spat over a cab with a rather disheveled woman who's toting a lot of camera equipment. They end up sharing the cab. "I bet you'd like my wife," he says. "You remind me of her a little." They shake hands warmly as he gets off at his destination. It's the last time they ever see each other.

Challenging Your Partner Means Challenging Yourself as Well

As Bernard discovered in our parallel universe, when you challenge your partner, you get challenged right back. When he risked pointing out that his wife was stagnating, she picked up the gauntlet and began to grow in unpredictable and disconcerting ways. She stopped catering to him, and he had to learn to fend for himself. As her life filled up with new people and projects, dining with her became a treat that he couldn't and didn't take for granted. As a result of demanding that Stacy be more fully present in her own life, Bernard, too, has been challenged to be more fully present.

Now, let's consider our other unhappy couple. Sebastian would have been taking a huge risk if he'd challenged Colleen about the self-destructive pattern that she was developing around sex. Asking her to look at her sexual issues would likely have led to a showdown in which Sebastian would be obliged to confront painful issues of his own. But that's not the half of it. Even to *contemplate* challenging Colleen would have brought

Sebastian face to face with his past—never mind how she actually responded.

Sebastian already knows that he had a lousy mother. Severe postpartum depression had prevented her from bonding with him when he was an infant, and she continued to reject him as he got older. She punished him severely and unfairly, cursed at him, and called him evil. On one occasion, she tied him to a chair and beat him with a broomstick. Sebastian, a veteran of years of therapy, is well aware of the damage this caused him and has done a lot of grieving over it. What he has never acknowledged or grieved, though, is that his father was a passive witness to many of these episodes of maternal cruelty. Sebastian never questioned this as a child. He needed to believe that he had at least one good parent. Far from reproaching his father for tolerating his mother's bizarre behavior, Sebastian concluded that this tolerance was the mark of a good husband and a good father. He admires and tries to emulate his father's ability to treat mountains as molehills. To consider now that being a good husband means confronting his own wife's destructiveness, Sebastian would have to admit that *both* of his parents had failed him. This would open up a whole new world of grief for him.

Sebastian is not unusual in this. To refuse to acknowledge bizarre behavior—much less confront it—is the norm in our society. What passes for normal in the average workplace and the average home is often downright pathological. Parents typically believe that they are "protecting" their children when they deny problematic or aberrant situations that are plainly evident to the kids. In doing so, they teach their children to ignore or deny their own perceptions. The tale of "The Emperor's New Clothes" recounts the universal childhood experience of being able to see what none of the adults around us are willing to acknowledge.

Odds are that something like that happened to you when you were a child. What that means is that you, like Sebastian, will come up against a familiar when you consider challenging your partner. The very thought of doing so will arouse fear and shame. Out of that feeling you will be tempted to start second guessing yourself. You may try to tell yourself that you're being too critical, that your partner's behavior isn't really so objectionable, that you, too, have faults, and so forth. Or you may imagine disastrous outcomes: your partner being outraged or crushed, an escalating series of conflicts leading to divorce. If instead of letting your mind run wild, you get in touch with your underlying shame, it will lead you back to times when you spoke the truth as a child and were either punished or dismissed by adults. You will need to grieve that memory.

Let's look at what might have happened in a parallel universe where Sebastian was able to confront his fears and go on to confront his partner.

"Colleen," he begins, "I need to talk about this new direction our lives have taken. Acting out fantasies has been fun for me, and that wouldn't have happened if you hadn't taken the risk of suggesting it. But I've been noticing that the further we go down this road, the less happy you seem. No matter what extreme we go to, you seem to want to push even further. I don't understand what you're after. I don't understand why you always have to pretend I'm someone else. To tell you the truth, it hurts my feelings. I don't want to go any further in this direction. Instead, I want you to tell me what's really up with you."

Colleen first response is to feel shamed. She feels as if Sebastian is accusing her of being emotionally disturbed and a pervert. His sudden attitude of detachment from the activities that he had appeared to enjoy makes her feel as if she is being observed and judged. It is shaming to consider that he's just been humoring her.

Shame is the most common reaction to being challenged. Your partner won't tell you that she's feeling it. The very nature of shame is that it is never expressed as such. Instead, it is expressed as some other feeling—indignation, hurt, or silent withdrawal.

Colleen chooses indignation. "You hypocrite!" she explodes. "You enjoy being kinky every bit as much as I do, and now you're trying to put it all on me. You're just losing your nerve; that's your problem. You've lost your nerve, and now you want to go back to being Ozzie and Harriet."

This outburst is distressing to Sebastian. He feels a
fresh wave of shame himself and is more than half
tempted to back off. But instead of denying it, he
acknowledges his underlying fear.

"You're right. I'm scared. I'm scared that if we keep
going in this direction, you're going to do something truly
dangerous and come to harm. I'm scared that you're out
of control. I'm scared that you will leave me if I can't
satisfy you sexually, and I'm beginning to doubt that I
can."

With that, Sebastian has articulated all of Colleen's
own secret fears. She is not ready to face them in this
moment. She blows up again and storms out of the house
before he can reply. Driving aimlessly, she has to pull off
to the side of the road because tears are blurring her
vision. First, it seems that she is crying because she is so
angry. Then, it seems that she is crying because she hates
herself. Sebastian is right: She is out of control.
Challenged to explain her motives, she realizes that she
doesn't really know what they are. It scares her to realize
this. It scares her now to recall all the crazy things that
she's done lately. The thought that Sebastian might
abandon her to her craziness scares her even more. But
gradually a feeling of comfort comes over her. He has not
abandoned her. He's not going to permit her to go on
acting crazy. Suddenly, she wants to go home.

The conversation they have when she returns is not
easy for Sebastian. She admits that she's not excited by him

and that throughout their marriage she has only enjoyed lovemaking when fantasizing that he was someone else. "You're so needy," she complains. "I can get you to do anything I want because the minute you think I'm unhappy with you, you get desperate. When you let me call all the shots, I don't feel like a woman. I don't feel like you're a man, either. You're just a needy little boy."

Now, it is Sebastian who is feeling shamed. His face gets hot as he recalls how he felt when she stormed out of the house. She's right: He was desperate. He'd have taken back everything he said just to stop her from leaving him. The phrase "needy little boy" opens in him a chasm of grief. She has confronted him with his familiar, and he feels awful.

Colleen, too, has been operating out of a painful familiar. Although she has pinpointed the immediate cause of sexual boredom in their marriage, she has yet to explore her own wounds. She has yet to ask herself why sexual excitement is such an urgent need for her that she is driven to perilous and degrading encounters, and why, if sex is so important to her, she chose to marry a man who did not excite her. The memory of being molested as a child is so distressing that she would rather act out dangerously in the present than face it.

When Sebastian imposes a moratorium on fantasy sex, she threatens to strike out on her own in search of a more accommodating partner. This scares him a lot. But he sees that the alternative—allowing her to violate his own limits—will be just as destructive to their marriage. Maybe he can't save the marriage, but at least he's not going to be the one to kill it. He holds firm. His own firmness surprises him. He begins to feel a new self-respect.

The healthiest part of Colleen wants an assertive partner and turns off sexually when Sebastian allows her to dominate him. But the part that is driven by her familiar chose Sebastian in the first place because he was willing to be dominated. The prospect of losing control over him triggers her own abandonment fears. It is the violent contrast between these two feeling states that makes her wonder if she's crazy. When she experiences the contrast, she panics and flies into a rage. Her tantrums are very upsetting to Sebastian. Although he doesn't depart from his anti-kinkiness policy, he is easily hooked into trying to pacify and console her.

One night, though, she doesn't throw a tantrum. She is stopped in her tracks by his quiet, confident refusal to be jerked around. "Sebastian," she says softly, with an air of wonder, "Do you have any idea how hot you are at this moment?"

He laughs. "Burn, baby, burn."

"No, Sebastian. I mean it. I really mean it. I'm not pretending you're anyone else. Who you are and what's actually happening at this moment is just turning me on something fierce."

We'd be kidding you if we said that Colleen and Sebastian lived happily ever after, even in our parallel universe. Both were severely damaged in childhood. Both have a lot of grieving to do. Nevertheless, their willingness to challenge each other has led them to discover a genuine spark of attraction. Learning to make love in the present has forged a new bond of mutual delight and given them an appealing alternative to the old symbiosis. All of this occurred because Sebastian took the risk of confronting Colleen's self-destructive behavior. Whether he realized it or not, this would inevitably lead to having to confront his own.

What Are You Allowed to Demand?

Most people would have no trouble considering Sebastian's demands legitimate. It seems entirely reasonable to ask one's spouse not to invite strangers into the conjugal bed. But the real Sebastian (i.e., not the happier one in our parallel universe) was unable to believe that he had a right to make this demand. He would have argued the "principle" that if he couldn't satisfy his wife, then she had a right to seek satisfaction elsewhere. Colleen, on the other hand, saw nothing wrong with demanding that her husband go to a hotel when she wanted to entertain a lover at home. If you were the referee, you might have called "foul" at that one, but that's beside the point. There are no referees in marriage.

Often, we try to serve as our own referee. Instead of simply making a demand, we get embroiled in an inner debate with ourselves about its legitimacy. This is rarely productive because familiars can distort our thinking in either direction. Sometimes our familiars want to make outrageous demands to satisfy insatiable hungers arising from the past. Other times they tell us that we have no right to make any demands at all and that to say what we really want is to court scorn and rejection. With all this emotional distortion going on, how can you know whether the demand you want to make is reasonable?

The answer is that you don't have to know. Ultimately, it's up to your partner to decide. If she wants to do what you ask, then she'll do it. If she doesn't, then she won't. Provided you're leaving her free to make her own decision, there is no such thing as an illegitimate demand. You can ask your partner to dye her hair blue if you feel that would enhance your relationship.

When instead of stating a demand, we get hung up on the question of its fairness, we're operating either out of the delusion that we can control our partner or out of the painful certainty that we can't. For Sebastian to demand fidelity was to risk the possibility that Colleen would leave him rather than concede. That is always a possibility if our demand is non-negotiable.

Most are not. A demand is not the same as an ultimatum. We'd like you to begin thinking of demands instead as conversation-openers, as invitations to deeper intimacy. Telling your partner what you want is telling him more about who you are. Your partner's response to the demand tells you more about who he is—and prompts you to learn even more about who *you* are. Your partner may ask, "What's up with you that you want me to dye my hair blue?" You'll be challenged to think about that.

When it comes to demands, our motto is: "You may not get your way, but you always get your say." The point isn't to get your demands met; it's to make them. People don't need to get every request met, but they do need to get every feeling expressed.

Personal growth has a lot more to do with changes in the way we feel than with changes in our external circumstances. For Colleen, the more drastically she altered her sex life, the more she felt trapped in the same old frustration. It was Sebastian's refusal to budge any further that finally prompted her to examine the feelings that were making her so unhappy in the first place. On the other hand, he would never have been moved to do that if she hadn't challenged him to engage with her sexual fantasies. Her challenge provoked the crisis that led him to challenge her in return.

You don't have to be right to challenge your partner. As Stacy went on to demonstrate, Bernard was wrong when he said that sculpting butter was not a suitable occupation for an adult. *He* might not care what shape the butter is, but some people are willing to pay good money to see food presented with imagination and flair. Nevertheless, Stacy herself would not have discovered this if Bernard hadn't challenged her. She was wasting her time trying to please him with elaborate meals, and she never would have faced this if he'd kept up the charade of pretending to be pleased.

Yes, he hurt her feelings. So what? Her anger over his reaction spurred her to change in a way that, ultimately, made both of them much happier. Truly intimate relationships can weather hurt feelings. And yes, Stacy stayed angry for a long time after that incident. Relations between them were strained for weeks afterward. Again, so what? Would you rather have a bad month or a bad life? Lifelong relationships can survive periods of strain.

We believe that most people grossly underestimate themselves and their partners. Human beings are much more resilient than we tend to imagine. Your partner will not have a nervous breakdown if something you say shocks, enrages, or offends him. He will not go jump off a bridge if you disappoint him. (If he does, then he has a lot more problems than you disappointing him.) Any marriage worth keeping can survive a great deal of upheaval—and will not be worth keeping if you don't risk that upheaval.

The great irony of the myth of unconditional love is that it becomes an alibi for never challenging conditions. What could be more *conditional* than a love that depends on never saying what you truly feel, never asking for what you truly want, and resigning yourself to being bored stiff by your partner for the rest of your born days? You will never discover the true depth of your commitment to one another if you don't put it to the test.

Your **willingness to engage** in conflict determines the depth and quality of your relationship.

reality

Chapter 6

In our last chapter, Bernard expressed his feelings in a way that you probably thought was tactless. The result was that his wife left the room in tears.

By contrast, Sebastian expressed himself in the way therapists are always saying that you're supposed to express yourself. Instead of judging Colleen, he talked about his own feelings. He made what is called an "I statement," the kind that goes: "When you do _____, I feel _____." Sebastian filled in that second blank with a full and honest account of his fears, for which he did not attempt to hold Colleen responsible. As therapists ourselves, we award him full marks for form.

The result was that his wife left the room in tears.

The formula for "I statements" can be found in countless self-help books, and couples all over America have been earnestly trying to apply it for the past three decades. Nevertheless, their conflicts still end in tears, yelling, and not speaking to each other for the rest of the day. Whereupon they conclude that advice from therapists on how to manage conflict simply doesn't work.

They're right if by "manage" they mean being able to have conflicts without ever getting upset. We'll admit from the outset that we have no idea how to do that. We ourselves are quite frequently upset.

Is that a problem?

You've probably been assuming so all your life. But stop and think about it. *Why* is getting upset a problem?

Consider your alternatives. You are disappointed with your partner. Disappointment is a gap between what you expected or hoped for and what you actually got. So, what are you going to do about it? Let's run through your options:

1. You can conceal your disappointment so as not to risk upsetting your partner. Your disappointment does not go away when you do this. Usually it turns into a grudge. Eventually—a month, a year, or a decade later—your partner will hear about it. It will come tumbling out along with several dozen other grudges when you finally explode.

2. You can express it indirectly by taking little digs at your partner, barbed comments that communicate your displeasure, without leaving your spouse any the wiser as to *why* you are displeased. This is an effective way of punishing your partner but does nothing to alleviate the actual cause of your disappointment.

3. You can hint or otherwise attempt to manipulate your partner into doing what you want without actually coming out and saying what it is. (Can you think of a single time when that has actually worked?)

4. You can try to talk yourself out of your disappointment, taking refuge in the familiar feeling that you can never really get what you want and

probably don't deserve it anyhow. While doing this, you will take on a sulky appearance, leading your partner to conclude that she's in the doghouse but leaving her clueless as to why.

5. You can come right out and say how you feel. This may upset your partner. You will go on to have some form of communication that, depending on how upset the two of you get, you will call a discussion, an argument, a tiff, a quarrel, or a fight. Whatever it is, by the time it is over, your partner will know how you feel and you will know how your partner feels.

The first four of these options leave you feeling upset to some degree without learning anything new about each other. The fifth option leaves you feeling upset to some degree while being fully present and engaged. If you are disappointed, then not feeling upset at all is not an option. Your choices boil down to either overt distress, which has the potential to enhance your intimacy with your partner, or covert distress, which will poison your relationship with untraceable hostility.

In other words, being distressed is not the issue. It is not a symptom that your relationship is in trouble or that you are communicating badly. It is, rather, a frequent by-product of communicating *well*. To be truly intimate requires setting limits, asserting boundaries, challenging your partner, and making demands. We don't know of any way to do that without experiencing some distress. In principle, you want an assertive partner. That doesn't mean you like hearing "No." In principle, you want your partner to challenge you. That doesn't mean you feel great at the moment he asks you to change.

Your Worst Quarrels Are Not about Each Other

You have probably noticed that the distress level in some conflicts is much higher than in others. Sometimes you and your partner are able to resolve your differences quite amicably. Other times, you end up chewing the scenery. The level of intensity has little to do with the quality of your communication skills. You may notice that sometimes you approach each other with great tact but still end up in a painful quarrel. Other times you're blunt yet manage to air your differences without hurting each other's feelings. Why is this?

The emotional intensity of a conflict depends on whether it is rooted in the past or in the present. Conflicts that are truly about the present are easily managed in the present. Those that resist resolution and arouse intense feeling are arising from the past and from your familiars. Your worst fights are not really about your marriage at all. They're about pain that you were feeling before you and your partner ever met.

When you are emotionally situated in the present, it is easy to come to agreement by consulting your shared values. Earlier, we described how a shared vision enabled us to decide where to relocate and to design our dream house without ever getting into a fight. Now, we are co-authoring this book and have managed to get to Chapter 6 without experiencing the slightest discord. Undertaking projects jointly is easy for us, and it's a great pleasure because these endeavors are firmly grounded in the present and in our identical core values. A client, contractor, or editor can speak to either one of us and get basically the same answer that he would have gotten from the other.

At the same time, we confessed a few chapters back that we once got into a major conflagration over chicken soup. A trivial problem in the present led to real anguish for both of us when we triggered each other's familiars. We have already described how Morrie's buried pain provoked him to blow up at Arleah. But if Morrie's familiar had been the whole story, then Arleah would not have stormed out of the house in the middle of the night, threatening never to return. Had her own emotions been firmly situated in the present, she would have reasoned calmly: "Morrie's anger can't really be about me or about chicken soup. I wonder what all this fuss is *really* about." Instead, she felt panic and fury. Those feelings were no more about Morrie than his original outburst was about her.

When we first told you this story, you may have wondered why Arleah had been submitting so docilely to Morrie's kitchen inspections up until the night of the quarrel. Why had she never questioned the premise that to meet his exacting housekeeping standards was her responsibility? And when she at last got fed up with it, why was she unable to state her position firmly and reasonably and leave it at that? Why did what she'd tolerated cheerfully for years suddenly look to her like grounds for divorce?

In Arleah's family, conflicts routinely led to ultimatums. With her dictatorial father, there was no possibility of discussion, compromise, or collaborative problem solving. The moment a difference arose, he declared, "My way or the highway." For Arleah as a child, docile compliance was the only bearable option. To challenge her father was to risk being rejected by him. This familiar feeling of helplessness felt right at home with Morrie's Inspector General routine in the kitchen. When he behaved like that, she felt the way that she was used to feeling, the way that she *expected* to feel. That side of Morrie attracted her—attracted the wounded side of her personality. So long as she submitted gracefully, she didn't have to face the pain that she had felt when bullied by her father.

When, on the night of the Great Chicken Soup Fight, Arleah finally balked, she felt terrified. Her childhood conclusion had been that she would lose her father's love if she stood up to him. Her familiar could not conceive of a happier outcome with Morrie. She threatened divorce because, as she saw it that night, ending the relationship was the only alternative to compliance. She was unable to perceive that, despite his blustering, Morrie would not reject her for asserting herself.

Occasionally, it happens that one partner in a conflict is operating out of the present while the other is in the throes of a familiar. One is calmly trying to solve the immediate problem while the other is reacting out of all proportion to it. This state of affairs is usually short-lived. A part of your attraction to each other is the uncanny knack each of you has for triggering the other's familiar. When your partner gets triggered, her intensity tends to trigger yours. This is how you can find yourself in the midst of a door-slamming fight over an issue you couldn't have cared less about when it first came up.

When Kate and Stan fought over the kitchen sink, Kate was, at first, emotionally situated in the present. Calmly she proposed the obvious solution: Hire a plumber. This sensible suggestion triggered in Stan a familiar feeling of inadequacy. He reacted as if she had deliberately insulted him. Had Kate been able to stay situated in the present, she would have recognized that his reaction had nothing to do with her or the plumbing and left Stan to wrestle on his own with the pipes and his familiar. But Kate's familiar finds it impossible to relax if anyone under the same roof is feeling distressed. When her manic-depressive mother reacted disproportionately to minor frustrations, it was usually a signal that a major depression was coming on. She could feel how much these episodes frightened her father, which made them even more frightening to her. As a child, her strategy had been to try to understand what her mother was feeling and to do whatever she could to pacify her. When Stan acted a little crazy about the leaking sink, Kate's familiar reacted as if he really was crazy. She is irrationally convinced that something terrible will happen if she can't make him feel better. Her anxiety feeds into Stan's anxiety, which feeds back into hers, and before long the plumbing hassle has escalated into a fight that makes no sense to either of them.

Getting to the Bottom of Conflicts

When one of our sons was fourteen, he got caught smoking in the schoolyard. We were both enraged. He looked at us calmly and said, "I acknowledge that what I did was wrong. But it seems to me that your reaction is out of proportion to what is happening in the present. Maybe you should look at why that is."

That is our own recommendation about conflict, in a nutshell.

The basis of any conflict is a gap between what you want and what you're getting. This gap does not lead to rage or crushing disappointment if what you want is arising from the present. If it's an adult need or desire, then your partner can probably meet it. And if she can't or doesn't want to, then you can either get it met elsewhere or live without it. That's why conflicts arising from the present are easy to deal with. Either you resolve it, or you agree to disagree.

When a conflict arouses strong emotion and when you feel as incapable of dropping it as you are of resolving it, the needs driving your behavior are coming from the past. Here are some of the internal signs that this is happening:

- Your need feels urgent. You feel like something terrible will happen if it isn't met immediately.
- The intensity of your feeling is disproportionate to the circumstances. A bystander might be tempted to ask, "What's the big deal?"
- Your partner can't fully meet the need even if he makes a concerted effort to do so. Nothing he says or does hits the spot for you. As far as you can remember, this need has never in your life been fully satisfied.
- Your feeling resists interruption. Once you get rolling with it, you can't seem to stop.
- When you are feeling this way, you lose flexibility and openness. You can't hear any new ideas, and you don't get any new ideas of your own.

- You can remember feeling the same way in other relationships. Your disappointment leads you to have negative thoughts about life, people, or the opposite sex in general.
- The intensity and urgency of your emotion leads you to do things that later you are sorry to have done.

Feeling this way doesn't mean that you're crazy. Anyone who was ever a child gets into this place as an adult. In other words, *everyone* does. What it does mean is that your feeling is not being caused by the present situation. Continuing to focus on what's wrong with your partner or what appears to be at issue won't get you anywhere. You'll just keep butting heads until you step back and investigate where your pain is really coming from. Beneath an anger that just won't quit, there always lies sadness. When you drill down to what that sadness is really about—and express it to your partner—what began as a fight becomes an opportunity to deepen your intimacy.

You might be wondering how we could ever quarrel when we understand this so well. Part of the answer is that we don't try *not* to quarrel. Although we know full well that the root of our quarrels is sadness, not anger, we don't try not to be angry. Emotions come in layers. Anger lies closer to the surface than grief. It is the emotion that you tend to experience first when a familiar is triggered by conflict. If you can't feel your anger, you won't be able to access your grief either.

Anger is the ability to act on one's own behalf in the present. It is how people experience their boundaries and how we distinguish self from other. In couples, boundaries have a natural tendency to blur. With the loss of boundaries comes a loss of intimacy. Paradoxically, the more you merge with your partner, the lonelier you feel in your marriage. When we are lonely, we want someone to be there who is *not* ourselves. Conflict is how you reassert your separateness, your otherness, so that the two of you can be intimate again. That's why sex is so great after a fight (in case you were wondering). If you withhold anger in order to avoid conflict, you never get to kiss and make up.

So the real question about conflict is not how to avoid fighting but rather how to move from anger to the kiss-and-make-up stage without wounding each other too much along the way. Here's where "I statements" and other communication skills come in handy. As we admitted in the beginning, these skills are useless if your object is to keep your partner from getting upset. You can't control your partner's response. Trying to control your partner defeats the whole purpose of having a conflict. What "I statements" are good for is keeping your attention focused on *you*. That's the only way you'll ever get to the bottom of what's bothering you.

Let's look at another of Kate and Stan's conflicts as an example. Both of their birthdays fall in September. Stan's comes first, and Kate makes a great to-do of it. She cooks him his favorite dinner or plans a fun date and presents him with an elaborately wrapped gift. Although she likes doing this for its own sake, she is also hinting at what she would like Stan to do when her birthday arrives two weeks later. It never works. Stan believes that generosity should be spontaneous. He seldom visits a bookstore without picking up something for Kate, and he presents his gifts unceremoniously. She finds a new title buried midway down the stack on her night table and wonders, "Where'd this come from?" That tickles him, and it pleases her too. But in all their years together, this delightful event has never coincided with her actual birthday. Kate spent the better part of a decade telling herself that she shouldn't mind before she finally got around to expressing her disappointment.

"Stan," she says edgily, "are you philosophically opposed to celebrating my birthday? Every year I knock myself out for yours, but you always let mine pass without doing anything special. It's like anything nice you do for me in the month of September is supposed to count toward my birthday. You do lots of nice things, but never on the actual day."

From these words and the peevish tone with which they are uttered, Stan is meant to infer that Kate is disappointed. He doesn't, though, because she hasn't actually said so. Her statement is all about Stan, not about herself. She asks for an explanation, and that's what she gets. Taking his cue from the word "philosophical," he goes on to express his ideological objection to scheduled acts of generosity. Kate attempts to argue but finds his rationale unassailable. As the argument wears on, she feels increasingly misunderstood while Stan feels increasingly picked on. Eventually wearying of this fruitless debate, they resort to exchanging insults.

"You're so hung up on ritual. That's your problem," he says.

"And you're just a meanie. That's *your* problem," she retorts.

This is a good example of how *not* to communicate. In trying to discuss the principle of the thing, Kate has gotten embroiled in a philosophical dispute that wouldn't get her what she wants even if she could win it. Meanwhile, Stan has debated his way into a doghouse that he can't seem to get out of. Because they've been arguing about an issue instead of expressing feelings, he doesn't notice that she's hurting. Not until he hears her crying in the bedroom does he realize that he's been missing the emotional point.

He sits down on the edge of the bed and offers her a tissue. "I don't get it," he says helplessly. "Why are you so upset about this?"

"I'm just being stupid," she sniffles. "I know it's childish, wanting you to make a production of my birthday. But I can't help it. I feel so sad when you don't."

"I see that, but I don't get it. Birthdays just aren't a big deal to me."

"I know. I wish I was like you that way. I always feel just awful on my birthday."

"Why?"

"Because I'm supposed to feel happy, and I don't. I can't. It was my mother who made birthdays happy. I guess because they made *her* happy. That was at least one day a year when I could count on her being in a good mood. We had all these family rituals. I know you think rituals are dumb, but I really loved them. Looking forward to them. Knowing exactly what to look forward to. Since she died, I never know what to look forward to. I dread my birthday now because all day I just miss her so much."

"Okay, I think I'm beginning to see it," Stan says. "You connect birthday rituals with feeling close to your mother, feeling happy together."

"Which, a lot of the time, we didn't."

"But on birthdays you did, and that's why they were so important to you. The rituals were predictable, while everything else about your mom was unpredictable.

Kate nods. "You know, I never really thought of it that way before, but you're right. That's it exactly."

Their first conversation had lasted nearly half an hour and gone nowhere. This time Kate comes to the heart of the matter in the first two minutes. Until she opened up to Stan, she herself hadn't realized that grief over her mother was the source of her birthday funks. Now all of a sudden, it seems obvious. The difference is that this time Kate is talking about herself, not Stan.

Emotions are no deep mystery. You don't need years of psychoanalysis to figure out what's bothering you. Simply asking "Why?" will usually do the trick. Kate hadn't been asking herself why, so Stan asked for her. This is a good move when your partner's intensity seems disproportionate to the issue at hand. Instead of trying to talk her out of what she's feeling, encourage her to delve deeper into where the feeling is coming from.

Heartened by Stan's willingness to listen, Kate came straight out and asked for what she wanted. "I would like you to give me a present on my actual birthday. Not a week before or a week after. On the actual day. And I want it to be wrapped in pretty paper and tied with a bow. I know that's silly, but it would really please me a lot."

"That sounds so easy," Stan said. "But for some reason, it doesn't feel easy for me. It makes me feel put-upon. I guess I really am a meanie."

Now, it's Kate's turn to ask why. "But you're not usually mean. You buy presents for me all the time. What's so hard about saving one for my birthday and putting some wrapping paper on it?

"I hate ritual. I hate it as much as you love it."

"But why?"

"In my family, if you needed socks, they wrapped up socks and called that your birthday present. Birthdays were nothing to get excited about. Birthdays suck," he concluded petulantly.

It takes two familiars to make a painful conflict. From an adult perspective receiving a present a few days before or after one's birthday is nothing to get bent out of shape about. From an adult perspective, being asked to bestow your gift on the actual birthday is likewise nothing to get bent out of shape about. But a request coming from Kate's familiar triggered in Stan a strong resistance that came from his own familiar. His response to deprivation in childhood was to suppress his desires, to tell himself that it was stupid and babyish to want something better than socks for his birthday. He can't respond generously to Kate's disappointment without acknowledging his own.

Once they recognized and expressed the feelings that were driving their conflict, Kate and Stan were able to resolve it. Kate realized that she had been expecting her partner to make up for the loss of her mother. No matter how hard he tried, he would not be able to do that. The loss was irreplaceable. Nothing to do for it but to grieve. She spent the first hour of her next birthday looking at her baby pictures and having a good cry. Wallowing in sadness first thing in the morning left her feeling quite cheerful for the rest of the day. In the evening, Stan came through with a wrapped present. His gift was an assortment of fancy wrapping papers and ribbons. Kate was delighted.

There is nothing wrong with making demands or expressing disappointments that are driven by your familiars. On the contrary, we believe that intimacy is best served by expressing whatever you are feeling, no matter how crazy you think it is. You do not in acknowledging that a demand is coming from your familiar waive all further rights to make it. Kate came to understand that Stan couldn't help the grief she felt on her birthday. Nevertheless, she still wanted him to wrap her present, and when he finally gave in, she felt happy. Her demand challenged him to face the grief that was driving his stubbornness. Getting into the spirit of her little ritual helped him to see that he had other emotional options and that he need not be limited by his own "birthday familiar."

Over the years, we've had a lot of good-natured conflicts about clothing. When we first married, Morrie was a sharp dresser, and Arleah—well, when Arleah really knocked herself out, she managed to look like a gypsy instead of a bag lady. She's prone to spilling things and couldn't see the point of investing in clothes that she was just going to ruin. As she put it, "Soup stains are my logo." This bothered Morrie a lot. He pestered her constantly to spruce up her look. When challenged to explore why her appearance mattered so much to him, he realized that he was coming from a familiar. The women in his family were not only stylish but also obsessively preoccupied with appearances. The exterior was polished in order to mask an interior sense of inadequacy. As an adult, Morrie was able to recognize the insecurities that drove their obsession with clothes and even to admire Arleah for her immunity to it. Nevertheless, a familiar got triggered for him when she didn't measure up to his family's sartorial standards. This was his own issue. It was not Arleah's responsibility.

That doesn't mean that the discussion was closed. Familiar or no familiar, Morrie still wanted Arleah to look nice. His insistence challenged her to look at why she was resisting so hard. That led her back to her own family's financial caution and her lifelong tendency to deny herself luxury. She realized that she didn't feel deserving of a classy wardrobe. Morrie was actually encouraging her to treat herself better. He was telling her that she was worth a lot and deserved to look it. She started buying nicer clothes to get him off her case and discovered that she enjoyed it. Had we allowed the conflict to drop when we realized it was being driven by our familiars, we both would have missed out on a lot of pleasure and growth.

When we encourage you to look into the old feeling patterns that are intensifying a conflict in the present, we don't mean to imply that this is a way of making the conflict go away. It is the intensity—not necessarily the issue itself—that is coming from the past. As you learn to distinguish past from present, you stop blaming your partner for your feelings. The conflict may continue, but you lighten up about it. You discover new options. Clothes will probably never mean as much to Arleah as they do to Morrie, but as she overcame the knee-jerk resistance of her familiar, she was able to enjoy dressing up more than she had expected.

Uncompromising Solutions

We're sometimes tempted to wonder whether our colleagues in the counseling professions started their careers as labor-negotiation arbitrators. Their typical intervention in couple conflicts is to hash out a fair settlement, a compromise in which each person gets part of what he or she wants and agrees to stop agitating about the rest of what he or she wants. This model works well for General Motors and the UAW. Applied to marriage, it is worse than useless.

Compromise is a lousy solution to any problem worth fighting about. Its real purpose is to put an end to the open expression of conflict, not to truly resolve it. Striking a deal about who takes out the garbage doesn't get to the root of why you're fighting about garbage in the first place. If it's taking you more than two minutes to figure out who should carry out the garbage, obviously something else is going on. It's the "something else" that you need to be talking about. Dispose of the garbage issue with a compromise, and the next thing you know, that "something else" will resurface in a fight over who gets control of the remote.

Compromise is also thinking way too small. It assumes that getting what you need and want necessarily comes at the expense of what your partner needs and wants. It assumes that neither of you can be fully satisfied. Based on this assumption, you go on to negotiate the degree of dissatisfaction each of you is willing to live with.

We believe that if you are operating out of shared values, it should be possible to resolve present issues to both partners' *complete* satisfaction. Values are an expression of your deepest and truest aspirations. They are a statement of how you want your lives together to be. If, like most couples, you are in fundamental agreement about your values, then you are in fundamental agreement about what you want. That being so, there is no reason why either of you should have to resign yourself to being dissatisfied.

But, you may want to argue, some issues are *objectively* hard to resolve. Take, for example, the decision to relocate. He is offered a great job in San Francisco. She already has a great job in Boston. They agree strongly that both of their careers are equally important. They agree strongly that neither should sacrifice his or her personal growth to the other. These shared values seem only to complicate the decision. How can they possibly resolve it without one of them making a sacrifice?

This type of dilemma is the result of believing that there are only two options to choose from: Either they move to San Francisco at the expense of her career or remain in Boston at the expense of his. If they remain stuck in that way of thinking, they are operating out of a belief that opportunities are limited to what's already been offered and that they do not have the power to generate other options. That's a familiar—a negative belief about the world arising from a child's genuine helplessness to obtain anything on his own initiative. It is not a realistic adult assessment of the world. In reality, this couple has many options. He can look for a better job in Boston. She can look for a better job in San Francisco. They can both look for better jobs in another city altogether. He can move, she can stay put, and they can take turns visiting each other on the weekends. Coming from a shared value of personal growth, they can continue to generate options until they find a solution that fully satisfies both of them.

As a general rule, either/or dilemmas arise from faulty thinking about the external world. If you and your partner are at loggerheads over a problem for which you can only see two possible solutions, then you're being confused by a familiar that's all but universal in American society. That we have the wherewithal to generate many attractive options is a relatively recent historical development. During the Great Depression and World War II, most people's options were quite limited. They were too busy just surviving to pursue genuine satisfaction. An assumption of scarcity has been passed down to most of us by our parents and grandparents. You may have inherited this familiar even if you were raised in an affluent home because your elders were living in the memory of hard times. The "scarcity familiar" views the attractive opportunity you're being offered in the present as the only one that you're ever going to get. It also leads to the widespread conviction that if you get what you really want, then someone else must necessarily be deprived. It isn't so.

Nevertheless, some conflicts do appear to be "winner take all" no matter how you slice them. For example, what do you do if one of you wants to have a child and the other one doesn't? This is a decision that will affect your lives drastically and permanently, and it doesn't admit of compromise. It would appear that no matter which way you go, one of you is going to lose big.

This was the problem that Miles and Janine faced when we first started working with them. It was the second marriage for Miles, a CEO in his mid-fifties, and the first for Janine, who was nearly twenty years his junior. She wanted to have a baby. Miles didn't. He already had two grown daughters and felt that he was too old to start all over with a new family. Both were worried that if Janine didn't become a mother, she would regret it all her life and come to resent Miles for it.

The attempt to avoid regret is a dumb motive for any decision. We pointed out that Miles and Janine would have to face regret regardless of what they decided. To remain childless would mean the loss of a potentially rewarding experience for both of them, and to have the child would require both of them to make personal sacrifices. Even if Janine and Miles were in perfect agreement, there was just no getting around the fact that sometimes they were going to be sad, and sometimes they were probably going to be mad at each other about being sad. Grief can't be avoided, no matter what you do. Fantasies about hypothetical grief are a complication that you don't need when making a major decision.

What Janine and Miles had going for them were identical and consciously held shared values. They were in complete agreement that neither of them should sacrifice self to the other and that both would need to fully embrace whatever decision they eventually made. But from there they were stumped. How could they reach such a complete accord when their desires were pulling in opposite directions?

Each of them had to work on the issue individually. For Miles, this meant exploring why he was so strongly opposed to having another child. He told us that he cherished the freedom that he and Janine enjoyed as a childless couple. He liked being able to travel at whim. He liked having Janine to himself. Bringing a baby into their lives would entail real losses for them. It does for every couple. But these sacrifices don't stop most married people from having kids. Why were they stopping him?

"Maybe because I know the potential gains aren't all that great," he said sadly. He confided that he was estranged from his two adult children. Parenting had not, on the whole, been a very satisfying experience for him. He didn't think he was much good at it.

Miles's divorce from his first wife had been brutal. The financial settlement had obliged him to dissolve a company, and later he discovered that his wife had, while still married to him, been having an affair with one of his closest friends. The trauma of this betrayal left him wary of committing to anyone else. He'd taken a long time making up his mind to marry Janine. Having a child would represent an even more solid commitment. To get in that deep scared him.

As he probed deeper, he acknowledged that he and his first wife had been estranged long before she divorced him. He had in this cold marriage replicated the estrangement he'd felt from his parents as a child. Having received little affection from them, he neither expected it nor knew how to give it to his wife and children.

Meanwhile, Janine was working to understand why having a child was so important to her. When the desire to have children is intense and passionate and when it is experienced as an obsession, unfinished business from one's own childhood is at work. We are unconsciously hoping that our own unmet symbiotic needs will be fulfilled by the symbiotic bond with an infant. Like many young women, Janine conceived of motherhood as being on the *receiving* end of unconditional love. Real children quickly disappoint this blissful fantasy.

Before they could make a decision about the present, both partners needed to grieve. Miles needed to mourn his lifelong sense of emotional deprivation. Janine needed to mourn the unmet infant needs that were driving her ardent desire for a baby. As they worked through their grief individually, the issue of whether or not to have a child became much less emotionally charged for both of them. Miles was able to see that it need not lead to the misery that he'd experienced in his first marriage. Janine was better able to see the negatives and to recognize that parenting was going to place difficult demands on herself as well as Miles. All things considered, she still wanted a child, but she no longer felt that she would be miserable if she didn't have one. She decided that Miles meant more to her than this desire and that she wanted to stay with him no matter what he decided. Soon after she came to that conclusion, Miles announced that he was ready, willing, and maybe even just a little bit eager to make her pregnant.

When his adult daughters learned that Janine was expecting, they expressed to Miles how jealous, angry, and ripped off they felt that he was starting a new family while neglecting them. Until then, Miles hadn't realized how much he meant to them. As a result of the crisis, his relationship to them has gotten closer. He has begun to discover new satisfactions in being a father.

Janine, too, has benefited greatly from her conflict with Miles. Had he readily agreed to parenthood, she would have gone into it with unrealistic expectations. These would have spelled trouble down the road. Through his example, she has learned to face and express her own reservations. This ability to communicate openly with each other about sometimes not wanting to be parents will serve their marriage well when the baby arrives.

Resolving their conflict took Miles and Janine nearly a year. It would not have been resolved as successfully if they'd tried to take it any faster. What they learned about themselves, each other, and parenthood grew out of the painful tension they experienced in that year. By hanging in with that tension, they came to realize that they would sometimes feel sorrow, regret, anger, and uncertainty no matter what they decided. Intimacy is not about getting rid of those feelings. It's about going through them together.

Compromise and other Band-Aid solutions are inspired by a desire to get conflict over with quickly. Conflict is uncomfortable. Sometimes it's very upsetting. But it doesn't mean that something's wrong with your marriage. On the contrary, a marriage without conflict is stone dead. If you can't remember the last time you and your partner opposed each other, then you are emotionally divorced. We'd be willing to bet that you also can't remember the last time you felt excited to see your partner, the last time she told you something that you didn't already know, and the last time you really cared what she was thinking.

Although it made us look pretty silly at the time, the Great Chicken Soup Fight strengthened our marriage. Morrie was able to discover and communicate what he *really* needed when he came home from a business trip and to lighten up a little about kitchen cleanliness. Arleah made the joyous discovery that she could stand up to Morrie without losing him. We had to rub each other raw before we could see how these familiars were unconsciously driving our interactions. We could not have learned this from any of the issues that we agree on or any of the decisions that we are able to approach without getting into a fight. Painful though it was, open conflict was necessary to bring our individual issues to a head.

Some conflicts persist for years, and some are never fully resolved. The presence of such conflicts is not, in itself, an obstacle to a happy marriage. It does not doom you to a lifetime of sniping and buried grudges. If you can remain curious about what your differences have to teach you about your own inner life and that of your partner, your conflict will become a source of fertility, enriching your intimacy. How a conflict gets resolved—or whether it ever does—is ultimately less important than how you relate to each other while you're having it.

myth

Spending lots of time together is very important.

*The best relationships are **low maintenance and high intimacy**.*   **reality**

Chapter 7

When they first meet us, some of our clients find us rather obtuse. Susan did. She was using the first session to prosecute her husband for neglect. Jack, the CEO of a rapidly expanding financial services company, also served as a board member for several arts organizations. The evidence against him included business travel two or three days out of every week, long working hours, and many late evening meetings. In the manner of an attorney resting her case, Susan concluded, "Jack has become a weekend husband. During the week, I might as well be single for all I see of him."

"Why is this a problem?" we asked.

Susan gaped at us. "What do you mean why is it a problem? Isn't it self-evident?"

"Not really. No."

We always respond that way to complaints about time, and our clients are usually taken aback. They feel that they have stated the obvious: that not having enough time together is the cause of their estrangement. We don't buy it. The only thing that lots of time together creates is lots of time together. It's no guarantee of intimacy. Complaints about lack of time are a signal that some other issue is at work.

"Well, for one thing, he rarely gets home in time for dinner," Susan explained.

"Why do you need him to be there for dinner?"

"Because we're married," she said, as if reasoning with a halfwit. "Being married means you eat dinner together."

"Why?"

"So you can catch up with each other, talk about your day, and so on. Most nights Jack gets home so late that we only have half an hour or so before it's time to go to sleep."

"And you have more to say to each other than can be said in half an hour? Sorry, I can't see it," Morrie said. "Jack's not that interesting, and neither are you. *Nobody* is so interesting that you need to hold a talkathon with them every single day."

"Being interesting isn't the point," Susan argued. "How a person spends their time shows where their priorities are. Obviously, I'm not a priority for Jack. His work is a lot more important to him than our marriage."

Work is one of those core values that cannot be sacrificed without a loss of self. As a value, it is not in competition with marriage. On the contrary, it is essential to a healthy marriage. The needs that are met by work are different from those that are met by an intimate relationship, and one is no substitute for the other. If Jack were to give up his work for Susan—or give it anything less than his best—then he would be coming to the relationship as less than a whole person. He wouldn't be happy and—just as importantly—neither would Susan.

Priorities are not the same as values. You might not especially cherish your car, but on the day it breaks down, getting it fixed probably becomes your top priority. You may consider your marriage your most important relationship, but the demands of a newborn infant will tend to take priority over time with your partner. Work also takes priority during the workday. However, if your partner became seriously ill, you would leave work to rush to the hospital. Your marriage would not, on that day, have higher value than it did before. It would simply have higher priority.

When couples first fall in love, they prefer each other's company to anyone else's. Spending time with your partner during the honeymoon phase is a high priority because you are laying the foundation for what you hope will be a lifetime of intimacy. It is also highly gratifying. You don't, at first, miss what you're *not* doing while hanging out with your partner.

This intense craving for each other, commonly known as "romance," eventually wears off. You begin to feel more relaxed in each other's company, and your interest in other activities revives. The longer you are married, the less time you need to spend together. You still need your partner's company, attention, and affection, but these needs are quickly met. If you're used to thinking that romance and intimacy are the same thing, you may interpret this loss of intensity as growing apart. It isn't. It is growing up. The single-minded focus on each other that nurtures your relationship at the honeymoon stage will seriously stunt your growth if it continues indefinitely.

True intimacy requires strong boundaries and constant challenges. You will not be able to challenge your partner unless you bring to the marriage experiences that your partner doesn't share. If the two of you always watch the same movies and TV programs, always socialize with the same people, always travel to the same places, and pursue the same leisure activities, you have nothing new to teach each other. Time apart is essential to your personal growth, which, in turn, is essential to the growth of your marriage.

Couples who have been married for twenty-five years or longer have the second highest rate of divorce. This alone should be all the proof you need that time doesn't beget intimacy. As children leave home and economic goals become less pressing, older couples suddenly find that they have all the "face time" with each other that they used to crave. Yet many find that all of these new hours spent together are lackluster. Time is abundant but empty. If the marriage has grown stale, then increased time together only makes that all the more apparent.

As we enter this phase of our own lives together, we are discovering some wonderful benefits. It's great to be able to make love whenever we feel like it and without having to lock the bedroom door. It's great to form adult friendships with children who are no longer dependent on us. But as the practical reasons for staying together have diminished, we are challenged to find new and deeper reasons. The older we get, the less we need anything from each other *but* intimacy. Had we not been cultivating that intimacy all along, our time together now would feel very empty.

Neediness: Then and Now

"I get what you're saying on an intellectual level," Susan said. "But it doesn't *feel* right to me. When Jack comes home late every night, I feel just awful. Maybe I shouldn't, but I do."

"Can I interject something here?" asked Jack, who had been silent until now. "There's not much I can do about my schedule during the workweek. But I've made a concerted effort to keep my weekends free for Susan. What bothers me is that it doesn't seem to have helped at all. If anything, my presence in the house seems to irritate her. We squabble a lot. And it seems that every night I *am* there, Susan spends the whole time complaining about the nights I'm not there. I feel like I can't win."

"Well, naturally," Susan retorted. "I can't complain that you're not there if you're not there to hear the complaint. If you were around more, I wouldn't have to save up all my complaints for the weekend."

"That's not much of an incentive to come home," Jack pointed out.

Maybe you and your partner have had the same circular argument. We see it a lot. The partner who is demanding more time seldom feels truly satisfied when she gets it. Frustrated that getting what she asked for has not made her as happy as she expected, she goes on finding fault with her partner, fishing for the source of her unhappiness. This is a sign that the needs driving the time demand are not coming from the present.

When you were a baby, constant physical proximity to someone who loved you was essential to your survival. Intimacy and physical togetherness were the same thing. They had to be because you were not yet able to draw conclusions about the present and future based on the past. For an infant, a minute is an eternity. If you found yourself alone in your crib, you had no way of knowing whether your parent would ever return. You also needed constant contact in order to establish your boundaries. Infants and toddlers, when left alone, cannot differentiate themselves from their surroundings. Only when being touched and talked to by a parent or other caring adult can they experience a sense of self. For a baby, being abandoned, even briefly, is like ceasing to exist.

If, as a child, you got all of the attention and affection you needed, you can handle solitude and separation as an adult. You developed a healthy familiar that trusts that absent loved ones will indeed return and that a need that isn't being met right this minute will be satisfied soon enough. Conversely, if you were deprived of the closeness you needed as a child and if your panic at finding yourself alone was not swiftly remedied, you feel needy as an adult. When left alone, you have trouble experiencing a sense of self. You crave from your partner the constant attention you needed as a small child. Yet if you actually succeed in getting it, you won't be satisfied. Your true needs as an adult are different. Clinginess in an adult is a symptom that you're losing touch with yourself. Spending time with your partner is not, in and of itself, a remedy for that. You don't need your partner. You need *you*.

Quality Time for Grown-Ups

In the movie *King of Hearts,* Alan Bates becomes involved with the inmates of an insane asylum and falls in love with one of them. At the climax of the film, he and she are watching a large clock. A catastrophic explosion will occur when the big hand hits the twelve. Bates's girlfriend is unconcerned.

"Don't you understand?" he says to her. "We have only three minutes to live!"

"Three minutes is good," she replies cheerily.

Three minutes can be very good indeed if you know what to do with them. The question to ask yourselves is not, "How can we find more time together?" but rather, "How can we be more intimate in the time we do have?"

When they hear the phrase "more intimate," many people (especially men) think "more sex." Men in our culture have not been taught any other method of cultivating intimacy. Many men seek sexual contact far in excess of the demands of their libidos because it's the only way they know to feel close. Women are, on the whole, not very receptive to that sort of thing. Sex as a substitute for true intimacy feels like a rip-off to them.

Women are more likely to equate intimacy with talking. Because women are good at talking, it is widely assumed (by women, at least) that women are better at intimacy than men. Many women have the idea that to be intimate is to do a "mind dump," telling their partners in one sitting everything that has happened since the last time they talked. Men are, on the whole, not very receptive to that sort of thing. Storytelling as a substitute for true intimacy bores the living daylights out of them.

Intimacy does grow out of conversation, but it's *how* you talk that counts. We have found that women need just as much coaching in how to talk as men do, and that, once coached, men are equally capable of keeping up their end.

The trick to intimate conversation is this: Instead of just telling each other what happened, tell each other how you are *feeling* about what happened.

Let's start with an example of how Susan usually talks to Jack:

"I went shopping for wallpaper today. Traffic was murder. It took me over an hour to get to the mall, and the air-conditioning in the car still isn't working right. I do wish you'd see to it. This is at least the third time I've brought it up. I was all sweaty by the time I arrived, and then I had to circle around for another ten minutes trying to find a parking spot. So anyway, I finally get to the store, and the salesgirl just leaves me standing there at the counter while she carries on with some inane personal conversation she's having over the phone. When she finally decides that she can be bothered with me, I show her my paint chips and fabric swatches and tell her I'm looking for a small floral print. She just waves her hand toward a whole wall of sample books and says, 'Florals are over there.' That's what passes for service nowadays. I swear, I don't know what's happening to the work ethic in this country. There must have been at least two hundred floral sample books, but does she help me narrow it down? No. So I stand there leafing through books for the next three hours or so until my eyes glaze over. I wanted to find

something that picked up the yellow of the woodwork, but not too much yellow. Just touches of yellow on a sage background. Well, it turns out that out of all those thousands of patterns, not one yellow matched. Some were too lemony. Others were two orangey. And most of the yellow florals were variations on daisies and sunflowers, which I find a bit trite; you know, a bit too 'flower power.' What I had in mind was something more along the lines of tulips or rosebuds. So now I'm having to rethink the whole scheme. What an ordeal!"

Jack nods dutifully from time to time to simulate interest in this scintillating monologue. When it appears to be over, he launches into his own.

"I know what you mean about service quality. You would think that if you order room service in a four-star hotel, the food would at least be hot. I waited nearly an hour for my dinner last night, and when it finally arrived, the fat had congealed on my steak and the sorbet had melted. Had to send them back, and by then it was too late to order anything else. Ended up eating all of the nuts and chips in the mini bar. The cable was out, too, so I missed the final game of the playoffs."

Is it any wonder that Susan and Jack don't feel close? They could talk like that until the cows come home without achieving anything remotely resembling intimacy. Let's look at what could happen instead if they shared what they were feeling about the events of the day.

"I went shopping for wallpaper today and got really frustrated," Susan begins. "It's funny that I always say I love decorating, because I was noticing today how much it stresses me out. I got totally fixated on finding this certain shade of yellow. Actually gave myself a headache over it. For some reason, I lose all sense of proportion over stuff like that. It's as if I imagine I'm going to be busted by the decorating police for choosing goldenrod instead of primrose."

"Yeah, I've seen you get like that," Jack replies. "You were nearly in tears when the new comforter didn't exactly match the curtains. Why is that?"

"I get afraid that I'm going to make a mistake. When people come to the house, I imagine they're judging me. My mother was like that—hard on other people's taste and afraid all of the time that they would be hard on hers. That side of her irritated the hell out of me when I was growing up, and now I'm just like her."

"I'd rather have ugly wallpaper and a happy wife."

"I believe you. Next time I get like that when I'm shopping, I'm just going to leave the store and go for a walk. Anyway, how was your trip?"

"Fine."

"That's informative."

"I don't really feel like talking about it. It was okay, but I'm glad to be home. Last night I felt lonely for you. Even luxury hotels get to seem pretty bleak after a while. For what it's worth, everything matches. But I'd rather eat tuna casserole made by you than filet mignon cooked by someone who doesn't give a damn about me."

Susan reaches across the table to squeeze Jack's hand. "I like hearing that you missed me. I missed you too."

In this conversation, Jack and Susan have exchanged fewer words than in the previous one. But with those few words, they've really connected.

Susan's unhappiness was implicit in her original account of her shopping trip. But all Jack could hear was a boring litany of complaints. No matter how hard he tries, Jack couldn't bring himself to care about the wallpaper. But Susan doesn't need him to. What she needs him to care about is how *she* feels about the wallpaper. When she comes right out and says how she feels, Jack doesn't have to struggle to work up an interest. Her story makes emotional sense to him, and he is able to respond in a way that satisfies her.

Jack's loneliness was buried somewhere beneath his rant about room service, but it would have taken Sherlock Holmes to detect it. When he shares that sadness directly, he gives Susan what she's been needing from him:

assurance that he values coming home to her. The entire exchange had taken no more than five minutes, but both left feeling close to each other.

To communicate in this way, you have to be close to *yourself*. Jack can't possibly know what the emotional point of Susan's wallpaper story is if Susan herself doesn't know. Before she could tell her partner, she had to stop and ask herself, "Why was shopping for wallpaper such a miserable experience for me?" Nor could Susan understand why Jack felt so disappointed with his hotel if he hadn't already probed that disappointment to identify its true source.

Women often complain that men "just don't get it" when they try to express their emotions. Usually this is because the woman is relating a series of facts and expecting her partner to infer from them what she is feeling. He can't know if she doesn't. The Y chromosome is no obstacle to understanding statements like, "I feel sad," or, "I feel proud of myself." It doesn't take a sensitive caring man to comprehend that "I feel angry" means "I feel angry."

If you and your partner are not used to communicating in this way, then we have a few suggestions to get you started:

- Look at your partner. Sounds obvious, but it's surprising how seldom couples make eye contact while conversing. Also surprising is what a difference it makes. Eye contact creates an emotional connection.

- Keep it short. Your partner won't be able to find your feelings in a long monologue, and you won't be able to find them either.

- Interrupting your partner's monologue is preferable to spacing out. You can say, "You're losing me with all these details. What is it that you really want me to know?"

- Keep it simple. Memorize these five words: *glad, mad, sad, hurt,* and *afraid.* That's the basic palette of human emotions. If you're not sure what you feel, try on each of these words until you find the one that fits.

- Ask your partner questions about his feelings. Don't try to tell him how he feels, why he feels that way, or how he ought to feel instead.

- Share your honest reactions by making statements about yourself, not your partner. Example: "I'd rather have ugly wallpaper and a happy wife." That will go over much better than, "You shouldn't get so stressed out over wallpaper."

- Your partner's feelings are not a problem for you to solve. Don't give advice or try to make her feel better. (Notice how quickly Susan arrived at her own solution when Jack left her space to think aloud.)

- When responding to your partner, say the first thing that comes into your head. Pausing to figure out the "right" response complicates things too much. If later you have second thoughts about what you first blurted out, then you can blurt those out, too.

The points we've just listed are tools, not rules. Making a conscious effort to apply them for awhile may help you and your partner break any bad communication habits you've gotten into. The most important point, though— the one to remember if you forget everything else—is that in order to communicate intimately with your partner, you have to know how you feel. The way that you find out is by asking yourself.

Not every interaction with your partner will be heart to heart. Sometimes you just need to exchange information: what time your child is due at the orthodontist, what the repairman had to say about the furnace, and so forth. But we strongly encourage you to catch up with each other emotionally at least once a day. We made that commitment to each other early in our marriage, and it has seen us through very hectic periods and frequent time apart. We both travel a lot in our work. Quite often we're only together at home one or two days a week—and much of that time we're entertaining houseguests. When we're apart, we catch up daily by phone. On average, our conversations only last about ten minutes. Those few minutes get the job done because we focus on how we are feeling about the events of the day and not a blow-by-blow account of everything that happened.

Ten minutes a day is pretty low maintenance. Your marriage can be low maintenance, too. The secret of high-intimacy, low-maintenance relationships is learning to separate the essential from the inessential, learning to come straight to the heart of the matter. That ability comes from staying in touch with your own feelings. The closer you are to yourself, the closer you can be to your partner.

Trusting your partner
is essential to a good
relationship.

It is
trusting yourself
that is essential.

reality

Chapter 8

A lot of people ask us: How do you know when to throw in the towel? How do you know it's time to end a troubled marriage?

The short answer is that if you're asking us, you're probably not ready to get divorced. When a marriage is hopeless, you know it in your gut. You also know it in your conscience and in your values. When your emotions and your values are in accord, you don't need anyone else to tell you what to do.

It is easier for us to describe the signs that a marriage is *not* hopeless.

You are not headed for divorce if you're fighting a lot. Not even if your fights are tearing you up inside. As you will have discovered if you've hung with us this far, intense conflict arises when a couple triggers each other's familiars. That is a very fertile situation for personal growth. People rarely work through past grief unless something is provoking a reprise of that grief in the present. Feeling intensely provoked by your partner is usually a sign that you are *right* for each other. Your familiars are a good fit.

You are not headed for divorce if you are dissatisfied with your partner. Being dissatisfied means that you still have vision. You can imagine your partner and your marriage becoming better than they are now. Only mediocre people are always at their best. You will not find a partner who never disappoints you unless you have *very* low expectations. Resignation—a chronic state of low expectation—is a far worse symptom than active dissatisfaction. Marriage thrives on mutual challenge, and dissatisfaction is the impetus to challenge.

You are not headed for divorce if your interests have diverged or if you have less in common than you once did and are beginning to spend less time together. This is a natural and healthy development in long-standing marriages and one that we encourage. As we hope we've shown you by now, neither shared interests nor constant togetherness have much to do with intimacy.

You are not headed for divorce if you feel less sexual passion for each other than you once did. In the natural course of things, sexual attraction waxes and wanes. As you grow closer, some of the intimacy needs that used to be met by lovemaking get met just by passing in the hall or exchanging a few words at the end of the day. At the same time, a willingness to challenge each other and engage in conflict has a way of periodically reviving sexy feelings that have grown dormant. Hot moments can suddenly arise just when you'd concluded that your lust for each other was gone for good.

The most serious danger sign in marriage is a conflict in core values. This is not easy to detect at first because many arguments that appear to be about "the principle of the thing" turn out to be driven by familiars and not by values. If the conflict produces a lot of emotional intensity, then it's probably coming from a familiar. A more telling symptom of a core values conflict is a loss of respect for your partner. Marriages can recover from loss of passion, periods of estrangement, and even moments of sheer hatred. But rarely do marriages recover from loss of respect.

A true values conflict can never be resolved because to give in to your partner about this issue would be to betray your own conscience. You will end up losing self-respect if you do that. In and of itself, unresolved conflict does not doom a marriage. You may be able to go on living in the inherent tension of agreeing to disagree. But values are so central to your vision of what your life and your marriage are supposed to be that a fundamental conflict in values becomes truly unworkable. You can't have a good marriage if you can't agree on what a good marriage should look like.

That conflict was at the heart of the trouble for one couple who was, in the end, unable to avoid divorce. In every session with us, Jessie had some new complaint to raise about her husband, Theo. Nothing is wrong with that. Complaints are a great starting place. The trouble was that Jessie could not move beyond blame. She left every session as convinced as she'd been at the beginning that Theo was the cause of her every emotional ache and pain. She took no responsibility at all for her part in their problems.

Jealousy was a big issue for Jessie. It didn't stop with Theo's female friends and co-workers. She felt jealous of anyone and anything that held her husband's interest for longer than thirty seconds. She resented his work, his children from a previous marriage, his hobbies, and his buddies. She felt slighted any time she was not the focus of his undivided attention.

Theo admitted that he often begrudged Jessie the affection and reassurance she craved. His initial response to her complaining was to withdraw. With a little prompting from us, he began to see that he had recreated in his marriage the familiar feeling that he was always in the wrong and that nothing he did was ever good enough for his critical, demanding father. As he worked through his grief over this, he became more open to Jessie, more willing to stand up for his own needs and also more willing to accommodate some of hers. He quickly learned to ask himself where his emotions were coming from and to share what he discovered with Jessie. Before long, he was taking full responsibility for his feelings and growing by leaps and bounds.

The trouble was that Jessie was not making a reciprocal effort to grow. When shown the connection between what she was feeling in the present and her familiars from the past, her first—and last—response was always, "Yeah but. . . ." followed by a redoubled effort to make the case that whatever she was feeling was Theo's fault. The upshot was that in this marriage, Theo was 100 percent responsible for himself and 100 percent responsible for Jessie. He was alone carrying the entire burden of trying to make the relationship work.

In Jessie's defense, we should point out that she had what is probably the most difficult familiar of all to deal with. She believed that she'd had perfect parents and a perfect childhood. That is not because she was repressing something dramatically awful. We've seen people who have been the victims of severe childhood trauma unearth and grieve terrible memories. Jessie didn't have terrible memories because nothing overtly terrible had ever happened. Her parents simply treated her like a perfectly nice piece of furniture in their perfectly nice home. She received neither anger nor affection. She received no particular attention at all. For a child, the worst thing that can happen is nothing. You can define your boundaries and build your character against an actively abusive parent. You can't define anything against a parent who doesn't relate to you at all. It is the worst form of parental abandonment, but it leaves its victims feeling like they don't have a case. Jessie's wound didn't bleed. It was just a big gaping hole in her heart. To face that kind of grief is very difficult and requires great courage.

We act with courage when we act out of our values. Had Jessie believed, as Theo did, that her responsibility in marriage was to face her familiars and grieve her own sorrows, she would have mustered the courage to do so. But Jessie did not believe this. Personal responsibility was not a value for her. Unable to recognize that she had been a victim of abandonment in childhood, she was intent on proving that she was the victim of abandonment by her husband. She simply would not let it drop.

Over time, the compassion that Theo felt for Jessie gradually gave way to a loss of respect. A person who is capable of taking emotional risks cannot, over the long haul, continue to respect someone who is not his equal in courage. The only worthy partner for an emotional adult is a fellow emotional adult. Theo was ashamed of this feeling at first and tried to talk himself out of it. But to live with someone who was not his true peer became very lonely for him. After a while, he was no longer angry, no longer tormented by their frequent upheavals, and no longer felt that he had any charges to level at Jessie. The relationship was simply empty. There was no particular drama around his decision to ask for a divorce. It gradually dawned as a quiet certainty that he and Jessie were already divorced in their hearts. When that happens, you just know.

The Myth of Trusting Your Partner

We have never ruled out the possibility that we might someday split up. Our willingness to contemplate divorce does not spring from lack of commitment. It is rather the *expression* of our commitment. We are fully committed to our shared core values. We hold those values even higher than our marriage itself. If either one of us ceases to grow, ceases to challenge the other, or attempts to stunt the other's growth, then we will have lost our reason for being together. Should our marriage ever come to feel empty in this way, we recognize that it would be time to part. As we see it, any relationship worth having is worth leaving.

You could say that our love is unconditionally conditional. This raises the question of trust. How do you fully trust someone if you know that he might leave you someday? How do you fully trust someone when you realize that her love for you is not unconditionally guaranteed? Our response is that you're not really trusting your partner *unless* you realize this.

Let's take a closer look at what people usually mean by "trust." You might say that you trust a friend in whom you are confiding a secret. What you probably mean is that you believe your friend won't judge you harshly for what you are revealing and won't reveal it to anyone else. You might say that you are trusting your spouse when you don't hire a private investigator to follow her around. What you mean is that you believe that your spouse won't cheat on you. You might say you are trusting your teenager when you turn over the car keys to him. What you mean is that you believe in the dubious proposition that your kid will drive safely.

In other words, what "I trust you" really means is, "I believe you will not do what would hurt or upset me." This is another way of saying that you believe you and your druthers have control over the other person. You believe that their actions will be motivated by *your* feelings and that your agenda is their agenda. If that belief proves false, then you consider yourself to have been betrayed. When you trust in this sense, betrayal is all but inevitable. The fact is that you *can't* control other people. If by "trust" you mean that you believe that you can, then you're much better off not trusting anyone.

Since no one lives very long without experiencing other people's capacity to do the unwelcome and the unexpected, a great many people say that they have "trust issues." If you've ever been in a relationship with someone like that, you won't be at all surprised to hear us say that what she actually has is control issues.

Take Drew, for example. After seven years of marriage, his wife, Sondra, fell in love with someone else and asked for a divorce. The part that Drew can't seem to get over is that he hadn't seen it coming. As Sondra tells the story, he would not have been surprised if he'd been paying attention. Over the years her complaints about their marriage had fallen on deaf ears. No matter how hard she tried to communicate her dissatisfaction, Drew persisted in believing that the marriage was happy because *he* was happy (or at least not unhappy). Because he felt blindsided by her decision, Drew concluded that his wife had been deceiving him all along.

After that, he started to have "trust issues" with everyone. He drove his subordinates nuts with his demands that they document their every move. As one of them joked, "If you call in sick, better come in the next day with the results of your CAT scan." Drew couldn't hire someone to paint his kitchen without requiring her to sign a three-page contract, nor would he put his own name to any document without having it reviewed by his lawyer. He never paid a restaurant check without first checking it with his calculator.

When he started seeing women again, Drew spent every first date telling the bitter story of how his ex-wife had betrayed him. If his dates had anything to say in defense of Sondra, he didn't ask them out again. They were the lucky ones. Those who were willing to feel as sorry for Drew as he felt for himself soon found themselves blackmailed by his vulnerability. He all but stalked them in his attempts to verify that they were faithful—calling late at night and driving by their houses for no other reason than to reassure himself that they were home and alone. When they complained, Drew pulled a mournful face and reminded them that he had "trust issues." Some felt sorry enough for him to tolerate this for a few months. But when solid evidence of their fidelity failed to appease his paranoia, even the most bleeding-hearted eventually ran for their lives. As his last girlfriend put it the night she broke up with him, "You've managed to convince me that I *will* cheat on you." With each breakup, Drew's conviction that women are basically untrustworthy grew more solid and unassailable.

Drew believes that his "trust issues" began with his divorce. Until the day that she announced she was leaving, he truly believed that he trusted Sondra. What he was calling "trust" was actually a form of denial. He denied that their marriage was unhappy and denied the possibility that Sondra would ever act on her own behalf. Unwilling to face her pain and his own, he tuned out the evidence that she was contemplating escape. Through denial, he was able to maintain the illusion that he controlled her. When she finally took action, it came as a shock. That is not because she had been deceiving him. It is because he had been deceiving himself. His "trust" was a resolute refusal to acknowledge pain. Having paid a steep price for this self-deception, what Drew was experiencing is a loss of trust in *himself.*

Adults don't die when they are unpleasantly surprised by another person's behavior. If you feel panic at the very thought that someone might deceive or abandon you, that panic is coming from when you were little and truly helpless to cope with such a misfortune. This is not to say that it doesn't hurt on an adult level to lose someone that you love or to find out that he has deceived you. Of course, it does. You'll feel awful if it happens. But if the thought of it scares you so much that you want to take out an emotional insurance policy, the intensity of your fear is coming from a familiar.

Drew's fear dated back to complications in his mother's pregnancy with his younger brother. Confined to bed rest during the final trimester, she placed him in the care of an aunt. He was too young to understand the reason for his abrupt exile or to realize that it was temporary. When he cried over the separation, the adults around him kept exhorting him to "be a big boy." That is how denial of his pain and anxiety became a familiar for him.

Fear-driven behavior has a way of provoking the very thing you fear. Through their suspiciousness and jealousy, both Drew and Jessie brought on the abandonment that they dreaded. When that abandonment became a fact, they felt all the more justified in their mistrust. Once you get this sort of vicious circle going, it is difficult to arrest it because the objective facts of your life keep confirming your worst fears. The only way out of the vicious circle is to take responsibility for it, to recognize that, through your own distrust, you are setting up other people to fail you.

If Trust Isn't Control, What Is It?

Trust is what you're doing when you know for sure that your partner will disappoint you and you don't let it hold you back.

Trust is knowing that your partner won't always respond the way you hope she will when you confide in her but confiding in her anyway.

Trust is knowing that your partner won't always give you what you want and asking for it anyhow.

Trust is sharing your honest reaction even when you know it's going to upset your partner.

Trust is raising a touchy issue even when you anticipate that it's going to lead to a fight.

Trust is challenging your partner's self-defeating behaviors because you know that he can do better.

In short, trust is taking risks even though you know you won't always like the results. You are willing to be vulnerable to disappointment because you treat every disappointment as an opportunity to grow. The more intensely you feel the disappointment, the more it has to teach you. From this perspective, you could almost say that your partner can do no wrong. Either she will do what you like or she will do what you don't like, and you will grow from the experience.

But isn't that just giving your partner permission to do hurtful things?

In a word: yes. It is. For what that's worth. (Are you imagining that he won't do hurtful things if he doesn't have your permission?) Marriage hurts no matter what you do. To express trust through risk-taking is to accept responsibility for that hurt. You are getting hurt on your own terms. When you consciously assume the risk of getting hurt, you are trusting yourself to handle it. That is the one form of trust that is never betrayed.

As Theo discovered, you might be taken advantage of by a partner who doesn't share your commitment to learning from disappointment. If you offer emotional generosity and your partner responds with exploitation, if you offer courage and your partner responds with cowardice, or if you take personal responsibility and your partner responds with blame, then you're married to the wrong person. Better find that out sooner rather than later. The only way to find out for sure is to take risks—in other words, to trust.

When you value intimacy, you don't give up easily on someone you love. Like Theo, you may be so intent on breaking the grip of your own negative patterns that you don't notice at first that your partner isn't making a reciprocal effort. While this is going on, you are indeed vulnerable to exploitation. But so what? There is no shame in giving a relationship your very best shot. If your partner can't or won't respond in kind, that doesn't make you a fool. What you learn from your effort to grow in a bad relationship will be a wonderful gift to the better partner you choose next time.

Trust is not about believing in other people. Trust is believing in *yourself*. It is knowing that whatever other people do, you can handle it. You might not like it, but you can handle it. If your partner lets you down, then you will feel awful for a while, but you will not feel awful for the rest of your life. If your partner betrays or abandons you, you will not jump to the conclusion that *every* potential partner is going to betray or abandon you. You will be able to dust yourself off and go on to love again.

You arrive at this kind of self-trust by way of grieving. When we are mistrustful, we imagine that the source of our fears lies in the future, in what might happen someday. In fact, the source of fear is in the past. That's the direction you need to be facing whenever you feel scared about what someone else might do. What you are scared might happen already *did* happen.

Jessie feared abandonment because she *was* abandoned, emotionally, as a child. Drew feared loss because he lost his mother at a time when he was too young to know that the loss was temporary. To discover that your worst fear has already happened is very good news. No matter how painful your past, the news is always good, because you're still here. You once hurt so badly that you thought you'd die. But you didn't. You survived that pain when you were little and helpless, so you will most certainly survive it now that you're grown.

The secret of grieving is that it leads to joy. It is the denial of grief that makes people miserable. If you don't face your losses, you can't get over them. When you grieve your losses, they lose their power to control how you feel in the present. You discover new emotional options. You are able to meet the future with confidence.

The more you are willing to risk, the more options you will have. You and your partner don't have to stay mired in the unconscious pact that you struck when you first got married. You don't have to remain stuck in the staleness, the boredom, and low-grade despair such pacts beget. Together you can liberate yourselves from the petty compromises that your familiars have driven you to make. You can demand more of yourself, your partner, and life than you ever dreamed possible.

With liberation comes loss. A healthy marriage is constantly evolving. To get to a new and better place, you have to move out of the place where you have gotten comfortable. To live zestfully in the present, you have to let go of a past for which you may feel great nostalgia. These are genuine losses. They hurt.

Marriage isn't about being comfortable. We can absolutely guarantee you that if you settle for comfort, your marriage will die. Even if you don't make it official with a divorce, you will find yourself living in the stuffy and sunless mausoleum of your familiars. You will never feel better than you felt as a child.

We hope that you won't settle for that. Both of us left comfortable unions for the constant challenges that we call our marriage, and we've never regretted it. We're having the adventure of a lifetime. After twenty-five years together, we're still capable of surprising each other. We're proud of that.

If we had to sum up in one word what makes a good marriage, that word would be *courage*. Love isn't compromise, sacrifice, or unconditional acceptance. Love is courage.

Index

Abandonment 9, 27, 28, 78, 79, 87, 88, 92, 99, 168, 169, 174
  emotional and childhood 51
  infant 79
  self- 88
Accountability and marriage 12–13, 18
Affection 47
Anger 45, 46, 125, 126
  and grief 58
Appreciation of accomplishments 49
Arguments 44, 45, 46, 47, 48
Assertion 86–87, 88, 98–93
Attention 47

Bates, Alan 152
Blame
  and grief 58, 59
Boundaries
  asserting 88–93
  finding 93–94

Cancer 44
Career 10
Care-taking role 80–81
Caring
  forms of expressing 46

Challenges
  to change 98, 99–104
  to partners 9, 15
Chicken soup 44, 45
Childhood
  disappointment 52
  feelings 27–30
  memories x–xv
Children
  and emotional abandonment 51
  and needs 50–51
  and self-blame 50
Commitment 24
Communication
  quality 13, 18–19
  tips for positive 158–160
Compromise 134–135, 142
Conflict 47, 115–143. *See also* Arguments
  arising from the past 124–134
  arising from the present 124
  and past experience 119, 120, 122, 123
  and present experience 119, 120, 122
  solving 123–143

uncompromising solutions
   to 134–143
and values 20
Contrast place 51–52, 56
Control 82
Conversation
   and intimacy 153–161
   tips for positive 158–160
Counselor 48
Courage 168–169, 179

Death 44
Dedication to life's purpose
   10–11, 16
Demands 111–114
   vs. unconditional
      acceptance 95–114
Denial 173–174
Depression 52
Descartes 86
Disappointment 46, 53–54
   dealing with 117–119
Dishonesty 77
Dissatisfaction 164–165
Distress
   overt vs. covert 118
Dysfunctional family 53

Emotional welfare 96–98
Emotions

expressing 158
substituting expression for
   58
Endurance 24
Estrangement 166
Excuses, making for others
   59

Familiar xi, xii–xiv, 27–30,
   31, 35–38, 48, 50, 53, 97,
   98, 119, 120, 122,
   131–133, 136, 142, 151,
   164, 165, 167, 168, 173,
   178
   and loss 52, 53
   "scarcity" 137
Family, dysfunctional 53
Fear
   confronting 106–111
   -driven behavior 174
Feelings
   avoiding 58–60
   pent-up 53
   present vs. past 60–61, 65
Forgiveness 24, 59

Goals 4, 5
Great Chicken Soup Fight
   44–47, 51, 120–122, 142
Grief 131. *See also* Grieving

expressing 56–63
Grieving xv–xviii, 56–65, 177
   and anger 58
   avoiding direct 58–60
   and blame 58, 59
   childhood 61
   direct vs. indirect 57–63
   and distractions 59
   and excuses 59
   helping a partner with
      62–63
   and histrionics 60
   past losses 65
   and when 63–65
   with your partner 62–63
Growth, personal ix–x, 7–9,
   14–15, 30, 167

High-intimacy/ low-
   maintenance
   relationships 146–161
Histrionics 60
Honesty 3

Ifs 33
Infant abandonment 79
Inner child 53
Inner renewal 11–12, 17
Intellectual achievement vs.
   practical

skills 49
Interest 47
   shared 2, 165
Intimacy 13, 85, 132,
   146–161, 165, 176
   high- vs. low-maintenance
   relationships 146–161
   in men vs. women 153
   and quality time 152–161
   and sex 153
   and talking 153–161
   substitutes for 81
   vs. neediness 150–152
   vs. romance 148
"I" statements 116, 126

Jealousy 82
Joy 177

King of Hearts 152
knowing oneself 158, 160

Life's purpose 10–11, 16
Limits, asserting 89
Loss 53, 80
   unmourned 63–65
Love 24–42, 179
   falling in 148
   vs. shared values 23–42
   unconditional 96, 97

Marriage
  and accountability 12–13,
    18
  and personal growth 7–9,
    14–15
  symbiotic 68–76, 80
    signs of 81–83
  and values 3–21
Mission in life 10–11, 16
Money 38–39, 44
Myths about marriage
  vi–xviii

Neediness 150–152
Needs, denying or dismissing
  50

Opposites 2

Pain, emotional 48
Parenting
  and disappointing children
    53–54
  and relationships with
    children xii–xv
Past experiences x–xviii, 41,
  42, 46
  and conflict 119, 120, 122,
    123

and positive affirmation
  49, 50, 51, 52
Past feelings 27–30, 35–37
Perceptions of reality 48
Personal
  dissatisfaction 82
  growth ix–x, 7–9, 14–15,
    30
  responsibility 33
Plumbing 48–49
Practical skills vs. intellectual
  achievement 49
Present experience
  and conflict 119, 120, 122
Priority of relationship 9–10,
  15–16
Problems
  personal vs. relationship
    43–66
Purpose 10–11, 16

Quality time 145–161
Quantity time 145–161

Rage 49, 78
Rejection 32, 33
Relationship, priority of
  9–10, 15–16
Relocation 44

Remorse 85–86

Resignation 164–165

Respect 165–166

Responsibility, personal 12, 17

Risks 175, 176

Romance vs. intimacy 148

Sadness 57
  avoiding 58–60
  confronting 60
Self
  blame 59
  challenge 104–111
  sacrifice myth 68
  loss of 147
Selfishness 83–85
Separation 44, 151
Setting limits and boundaries vs. selflessness 67–94
Sex 153
Sexual
  fantasies 73–76
  passion 165, 166
Shame 85, 86–88, 89
Solitude 151
Spirituality 11. *See also* Inner renewal
Standards 19

Symbiotic
  marriage 68–76, 79, 80
    signs of 81–83
    needs 79–80

Taboos 84, 85
Talking
  and intimacy 153–161
  tips for positive 158–160
Temperaments, shared and opposite 2
Ten-Point Checklist of Kitchen Cleanliness 44–45
Time
  quantity vs. quality 145–161
Tolerance 24
Trust 164–179
  and control 171–174
  issues 171–174
  and risk 175
Turner, Tina 24

Values 3–21, 30–42, 86, 87, 93, 135,
  conflict in 20, 165–169
  core 1–22

and difficult decisions   Virility, challenge to
    38–39   49
definition of 3   Vision, shared 41
and marriage 3–21
need for identical 3   Wants vs. needs 123–124
shared vs. love 23–42   Work 147

About the Authors

Morrie Shechtman is a personal and corporate consultant with 30 years of experience. Morrie's academic background includes an M.S.W. with a clinical specialization in psychotherapy. He also has his A.C.S.W., the professional credential required for independent practice. He has taught at distinguished universities throughout the United States, has worked as a therapist and counselor, and now also runs a successful management consulting company, Fifth Wave Leadership.

Morrie's first book, *Working Without a Net: How to Survive and Thrive in Today's High Risk Business World* (1994), is widely used as a reference in corporate America. It is utilized as a textbook by a number of universities and is used by many government agencies in management development training.

Morrie's second book, *Fifth Wave Leadership: The Internal Frontier* (2003; Facts on Demand Press; ISBN: 1-889150-38-X; $19.95), is available at booksellers nationwide.

Arleah Shechtman is a psychotherapist with 25 years of experience counseling individuals in committed relationships. Arleah's academic background includes an associate's degree in business mid-management, an undergraduate degree in Organizational Development and an M.S.W. with a clinical specialization. She also has her A.C.S.W., the professional credential required for independent practice. Her continuing education has focused on work with adolescents, work with small groups, and work with people experiencing grief and loss.

Acknowledgments

We wrote this book for two reasons. First, because we were urged to do so by a number of couples we have worked with over the years who felt that their experiences at our couples' retreats were profoundly impactful and life-changing. They felt that the values and principles that underpin our work should be shared with a wider audience and that other couples could gain much from our approach to building great relationships.

Second, we felt a responsibility to offer an alternative to the dreadful prevailing doctrine about intimate relationships being promulgated by the majority of those involved in the "helping professions." It is nothing less than shameful that these individuals refuse to own their bias and continue to present their work with others as an objective, "clinical" venture. These professions still cling to the patronizing medical model view of consumers: treat them with the fragility of emotional china dolls; don't confront obvious contradictions and evasions; and, worst of all, avoid rendering judgments that give people the badly needed impetus and catalyst for making fundamental changes in their lives. These unarticulated assumptions put into practice have left large numbers of people who have sought assistance with their relationships feeling either clueless about what to do, or feeling like failures. They have attempted to act on feedback and input that encourages them to compromise their core belief systems, settle for mediocrity in their most important relationships, and avoid making tough decisions. None of this has left them feeling any better about themselves or their relationships. We have no need to prevent bad advice from being offered to consumers of professional services. We *would like* that advice directly and openly articulated along with the underlying values, belief systems, and biases. This would allow consumers to make informed choices about who they'd like to work with and why they'd make that decision. This book is an attempt to bring some openness and sunlight to this process.

This book would not have been possible without the courageous commitment of hundreds of individuals who chose to work on themselves in order to grow their relationships with their life partners. We have learned much from them, and we owe them a large debt of gratitude. A number of these couples are referenced in the book. For obvious reasons, their identities are disguised and their real names are not used.

The title for the book came out of a discussion with Joe Spieler, a literary agent from New York. Joe gave us much input about the book, and his suggestions about possible titles eventually led to our landing on the final choice.

Our relationship with Jim Bull, president of Bull Publishing, has been a true pleasure. It would be an understatement to say that things have gone smoothly. If the measure of a good working relationship is that all the big, tough decisions were easy, then this has been an excellent relationship.

The solidification of our experiences and ideas into a book would not have taken place when it did were it not for our relationship with Celia Rocks. We met Celia, who is a publicist and marketing consultant out of Pittsburgh, about a year and a half ago. At our first meeting, Celia introduced herself, briefly described what she and her partner Dottie DeHart do, and then proceeded to tell us how boring and awful the first draft of our book was. We knew then that we liked Celia, and we'd work well together.

Our book would not have been written, literally, without Catherine MacCoun. Catherine is an extraordinary writer, and she did an amazing job of capturing our ideas, our experiences, and our "voice." She has superb organizational skills, in addition to her writing skills, and she made the writing of the book easy, effortless, and surprisingly quick. In addition to admiring her professional expertise, we have great respect for Catherine's commitment to her life partner, and the manner in which she was there for him, and herself, during his terrible illness and recent death.

Even with all this wonderful encouragement and help, the writing of a book is a time-consuming and energy-absorbing venture. It requires much support and assistance or the process can become overwhelming. A great deal of that came from Pam Brauer, the firm's practice administrator and Morrie's assistant, and Marilyn Kun, Arleah's assistant and our personal life manager. In spite of our crazy schedules and often frenetic pace, Pam and Marilyn keep us sane, organized, and mostly coherent. Without them, we would have little chance or opportunity to fully enjoy both our work and our home and personal retreat in Montana.

Lastly, we want to acknowledge Bob Kerrigan, our longtime friend and professional colleague. Besides being a business legend in the financial services and insurance industry, Bob has been an enormous contributor to our knowledge base and to the articulation of that body of knowledge in a variety of real-life settings. He has not only helped and encouraged us; he has always been in our corner. For that, we are more than grateful.

We would be remiss if we did not mention our own relationship. When we met each other twenty-five years ago, our lives began anew. Neither of us had believed, prior to our finding each other, that life could offer so much challenge, fascination and enjoyment. It was electrifying to realize that we had a common bond of learning, exploring, and growing. That bond has never diminished for us. We hope that you find that same joy in your relationship.

Morrie and Arleah

Ready to Move Your Relationships— Personal and Professional—Into the Next Frontier?

Explore These Products & Services Available from Morrie & Arleah Shechtman and Fifth Wave Leadership

Relationship Retreats

Co-authors Morrie and Arleah Shechtman offer couples' retreats. During a weekend stay in Montana, couples learn about all the concepts covered in *Love in the Present Tense*. Please call for a brochure on the retreat.

Executive Coaching

Exploring the critical tools of self-discovery and personal growth is the purpose of this one-on-one coaching experience with co-author Arleah Shechtman. Arleah provides a structured program of targeted feedback, regular and ongoing troubleshooting, and consistently updated action plans.

One-Day Fifth Wave Leadership Seminar

The blending of career and family life is integral to being a happy and productive person. Help your business team learn the basic principles of personal and professional success in the internally-focused Fifth Wave, as well as how to apply them. This intensive one-day seminar may be held at your place of business or at an outside location, depending on the number of participants and other factors.

Fifth Wave Leadership CDs

Gain from the insight of Morrie Shechtman at your own convenience and on your own timetable. Though new subjects are always in development, the following CDs are currently available:

Caring Feedback: Telling the Hard Truth

Understanding Your Familiars and How They Are Holding You Back

Picking Winners and Keepers: Targeted Recruiting in the New Economy

There is a substantial discount for bulk orders, so get one for every member of your team! CDs are available from our website or our office.

Morrie Shechtman's Books

You've read *Love in the Present Tense*; now read the book *Fifth Wave Leadership: The Internal Frontier*, and watch even more positive changes occur in your life. Morrie's first book, *Working Without a Net: How to Survive and Thrive in Today's High-Risk Business World*, is also available. Order your copy of *Fifth Wave Leadership: The Internal Frontier* and *Working Without a Net: How to Survive and Thrive in Today's High-Risk Business World* from the Internet, our website, or our office.

Morrie Shechtman's Keynote Speeches

A highly sought-after speaker, Morrie has lectured on personal transformation and productivity to audiences throughout the world. In his dynamic speeches, he pinpoints and elaborates on key messages that will take your business, career, and life to rewarding new heights.

Morrie Shechtman Presents "Creating a Conscious Culture"

Enjoy a "front row seat" with this classic presentation that introduces you to The Fifth Wave. Order a copy on DVD from our website or our office.

Executive Leadership and Cultural Development Program

This experience helps management teams achieve deeper levels of self-information and relationship building. By clarifying values, overcoming blockers, and eliminating destructive conflict, participants will be better able to negotiate their companies through the potentially dangerous waters of today's new economy. The program, facilitated by senior consultants of Fifth Wave Leadership, is structured into three processes designed to effectively prepare an organization to be responsive to the demands and opportunities found in a world of unrelenting change and competitive challenge.

Fifth Wave High-Performance Accountability Groups

This is a structured vehicle for identifying and removing long-standing blockers to heightened professional achievement and highly-fulfilling and meaningful quality of life. All groups range in size from eight to twelve participants and are facilitated by senior consultants of Fifth Wave Leadership. Accountability groups normally meet once a month over the course of one year.

For more information on any of these products, services, or events, please contact Pam Brauer at 800-807-5906 or please visit www.MorrieandArleah.com and www.fifthwaveleadership.com.

Fifth Wave Leadership is committed to doing everything possible to help you thrive personally and professionally in the 21st century.